PLUM
PUDDING

PLUM PUDDING

Of divers Ingredients, Discreetly Blended & Seasoned

By Christopher Morley

And merrily embellished by WALTER JACK DUNCAN

Printed at *GARDEN CITY, NEW YORK*, by DOUBLEDAY, PAGE & CO'Y and are to be sold by *All Worthy Booksellers, together with* OTHER VVORKS *by the Same Author, thⱱs modestly* offered to your Attention

1922

THIS BOOK IS DEDICATED
TO
DAVID WILLIAM BONE
DON MARQUIS
SIMEON STRUNSKY
MEMBERS OF THE
THREE HOURS FOR LUNCH CLUB

Almost all these sketches were originally published in the New York *Evening Post* and the *Literary Review*. One comes from *The Outlook*, one from *The Atlantic Monthly*, one from the *Haverford Alumni Quarterly*, and one from the Philadelphia *Evening Public Ledger*. The author is indebted to these publishers for permission to reprint.

Roslyn, Long Island
July, 1921

CONTENTS

[vii]

Contents

PLUM
PUDDING

THE PERFECT READER

ON CHRISTMAS EVE, while the Perfect Reader sits in his armchair immersed in a book—so absorbed that he has let the fire go out—I propose to slip gently down the chimney and leave this tribute in his stocking. It is not a personal tribute. I speak, on behalf of the whole fraternity of writers, this word of gratitude—and envy.

No one who has ever done any writing, or has any ambition toward doing so, can ever be a Perfect Reader. Such a one is not disinterested. He reads, inevitably, in a professional spirit. He does not surrender himself with complete willingness of enjoyment. He reads "to

see how the other fellow does it"; to note the turn of a
phrase, the cadence of a paragraph; carrying on a constant subconscious comparison with his own work.
He broods constantly as to whether he himself, in some
happy conjuncture of quick mind and environing silence
and the sudden perfect impulse, might have written
something like that. He is (poor devil) confessedly
selfish. On every page he is aware of his own mind
running with him, tingling him with needle-pricks of
conscience for the golden chapters he has never written.
And so his reading is, in a way, the perfection of exquisite misery—and his writing also. When he writes,
he yearns to be reading; when he reads, he yearns to
be writing.

But the Perfect Reader, for whom all fine things are
written, knows no such delicate anguish. When he
reads, it is without any *arrière pensée*, any twingeing
consciousness of self. I like to think of one Perfect
Reader of my acquaintance. He is a seafaring man,
and this very evening he is in his bunk, at sea, the day's
tasks completed. Over his head is a suitable electric
lamp. In his mouth is a pipe with that fine wine-dark
mahogany sheen that resides upon excellent briar of
many years' service. He has had (though I speak only
by guess) a rummer of hot toddy to celebrate the greatest of all Evenings. At his elbow is a porthole, brightly
curtained with a scrap of clean chintz, and he can hear
the swash of the seas along his ship's tall side. And
now he is reading. I can see him reading. I know
just how his mind feels! Oh, the Perfect Reader!
There is not an allusion that he misses; in all those

The Perfect Reader

lovely printed words he sees the subtle secrets that a lesser soul would miss. He (bless his heart!) is not thinking how he himself would have written it; his clear, keen, outreaching mind is intent only to be one in spirit with the invisible and long-dead author. I tell you, if there is anywhere a return of the vanished, it is then, at such moments, over the tilted book held by the Perfect Reader.

And how quaint it is that he should diminish himself so modestly. "Of course" (he says), "I'm only a Reader, and I don't know anything about writing——" Why, you adorable creature, *You* are our court of final appeal, you are the one we come to, humbly, to know whether, anywhere in our miserable efforts to set out our unruly hearts in parallel lines, we have done an honest thing. What do we care for what (most of) the critics say? They (we know only too well) are not criticising *us*, but, unconsciously, themselves. They skew their own dreams into their comment, and blame us for not writing what they once wanted to. You we can trust, for you have looked at life largely and without pettifogging qualms. The parallel lines of our eager pages meet at Infinity—that is, in the infinite understanding and judgment of the Perfect Reader.

The enjoyment of literature is a personal communion; it cannot be outwardly instilled. The utmost the critic can do is read the marriage service over the reader and the book. The union is consummated, if at all, in secret. But now and then there comes up the aisle a new Perfect Reader, and all the ghosts of literature wait for him, starry-eyed, by the altar. And as long as there are Perfect Readers, who read with passion, with glory, and then speed to tell their friends, there will always be, ever and anon, a Perfect Writer.

And so, dear Perfect Reader, a Merry Christmas to you and a New Year of books worthy your devotion! When you revive from that book that holds you in spell, and find this little note on the cold hearth, I hope you may be pleased.

THE AUTOGENESIS OF A POET

THE mind trudges patiently behind the senses. Day by day a thousand oddities and charms outline themselves tenderly upon consciousness, but it may be long before understanding comes with brush and colour to fill in the tracery. One learns nothing until he rediscovers it for himself. Every now and then, in reading, I have come across something which has given me the wild surmise of pioneering mingled with the faint magic of familiarity—for instance, some of the famous dicta of Wordsworth and Coleridge and Shelley about poetry. I realized, then, that a teacher had told me these things in my freshman year at college—fifteen years ago. I jotted them down at that time, but they were mere catchwords. It had taken me fifteen years of vigorous living to overhaul those

[5]

catchwords and fill them with a meaning of my own. The two teachers who first gave me some suspicion of what lies in the kingdom of poetry—who gave "so sweet a prospect into the way as will entice any man to enter into it"—are both dead. May I mention their names?—Francis B. Gummere and Albert Elmer Hancock, both of Haverford College. I cannot thank them as, now, I would like to. For I am (I think) approaching a stage where I can somewhat understand and relish the things of which they spoke. And I wonder afresh at the patience and charity of those who go on lecturing, unabated in zest, to boys of whom one in ten may perhaps, fifteen years later, begin to grasp their message.

In so far as any formal or systematic discipline of thought was concerned, I think I may say my education was a complete failure. For this I had only my own smattering and desultory habit of mind to blame and also a vivid troublesome sense of the beauty of it all. The charm of the prismatic fringe round the edges made juggling with the lens too tempting, and a clear persistent focus was never attained. Considered (oddly enough) by my mates as the pattern of a diligent scholar, I was in reality as idle as the idlest of them, which is saying much; though I confess that my dilettantism was not wholly disreputable. My mind excellently exhibited the Heraclitean doctrine: a constant flux of information passed through it, but nothing remained. Indeed, my senses were so continually crammed with new enchanting impressions, and every field of knowledge seemed so alluring, it was not strange I made little progress in any.

Perhaps it was unfortunate that both in America and in England I found myself in a college atmosphere of extraordinary pictorial charm. The Arcadian loveliness of the Haverford campus and the comfortable simplicity of its routine; and then the hypnotizing beauty and curiosity and subtle flavour of Oxford life (with its long, footloose, rambling vacations)—these were aptly devised for the exercise of the imagination, which is often a gracious phrase for loafing. But these surroundings were too richly entertaining, and I was too green and soft and humorous (in the Shakespearean sense) to permit any rational continuous plan of study. Like the young man to whom Coleridge addressed a poem of rebuke, I was abandoned, a greater part of the time, to "an Indolent and Causeless Melancholy"; or to its partner, an excessive and not always tasteful mirth. I spent hours upon hours, with little profit, in libraries, flitting aimlessly from book to book. With something between terror and hunger I contemplated the opposite sex. In short, I was discreditable and harmless and unlovely as the young Yahoo can be. It fills me with amazement to think that my preceptors must have seen, in that ill-conditioned creature, some shadow of human semblance, or how could they have been so uniformly kind?

Our education—such of it as is of durable importance—comes haphazard. It is tinged by the enthusiasms of our teachers, gleaned by suggestions from our friends, prompted by glimpses and footnotes and margins. There was a time, I think, when I hung in tender equilibrium among various possibilities. I was enamoured of mathematics and physics: I went far enough in the latter to be appointed undergraduate assistant in the college laboratory. I had learned, by my junior year, exploring the charms of integral calculus, that there is no imaginable mental felicity more serenely pure than suspended happy absorption in a mathematical problem. Of course I attained no higher than the dregs of the subject; on that grovelling level I would still (in Billy Sunday's violent trope) have had to climb a tree to look a snake in the eye; but I could see that for the mathematician, if for any one, Time stands still withal; he is winnowed of vanity and sin. French, German, and Latin, and a hasty tincture of Xenophon and Homer (a mere lipwash of Helicon) gave me a zeal for philology and the tongues. I was a member in decent standing of the college classical club, and visions of life as a professor of languages seemed to me far from unhappy. A compulsory course in philosophy convinced me that there was still much to learn; and I had a delicious hallucination in which I saw myself compiling a volume of commentaries on the various systems of this queen of sciences. "The Grammar of Agnostics," I think it was to be called: it would be written in a neat and comely hand on thousands of pages of pure white foolscap: I saw myself adding to it night by night, working *ohne Hast, ohne Rast*. And there were other careers, too, as statesman, philanthropist, diplomat, that I considered not beneath my horo-

The Autogenesis of a Poet

scope. I spare myself the careful delineation of these projects, though they would be amusing enough.

But beneath these preoccupations another influence was working its inward way. My paramount interest had always been literary, though regarded as a gentle diversion, not degraded to a bread-and-butter concern. Ever since I had fallen under the superlative spell of R. L. S., in whom the cunning enchantment of the written word first became manifest, I had understood that books did not grow painlessly for our amusement, but were the issue of dexterous and intentional skill. I had thus made a stride from Conan Doyle, Cutcliffe Hyne, Anthony Hope, and other great loves of my earliest teens; those authors' delicious mysteries and picaresques I took for granted, not troubling over their method; but in Stevenson, even to a schoolboy the conscious artifice and nicety of phrase were puzzlingly apparent. A taste for literature, however, is a very different thing from a determination to undertake the art in person as a means of livelihood. It takes brisk stimulus and powerful internal fevers to reduce a healthy youth to such a contemplation. All this is a long story, and I telescope it rigorously, thus setting the whole matter, perhaps, in a false proportion. But the central and operative factor is now at hand.

There was a certain classmate of mine (from Chicago) whose main devotion was to scientific and engineering studies. But since his plan embraced only two years at college before "going to work," he was (in the fashion traditionally ascribed to Chicago) speeding up the cultural knick-knacks of his education. So, in our freshman year, he was attending a course on "English Poets of the Nineteenth Century," which was, in the regular schedule of things, reserved for sophomores (supposedly riper for matters of feeling). Now I was living in a remote dormitory on the outskirts of the wide campus (that other Eden, demi-paradise, that happy breed of men, that little world!) some distance from the lecture halls and busy heart of college doings. It was the custom of those quartered in this colonial and sequestered outpost to make the room of some central classmate a base for the day, where books might be left between lectures, and so on. With the Chicagoan, whom we will call "J——," I had struck up a mild friendship; mostly charitable on his part, I think, as he was from the beginning one of the most popular and influential men in the class, whereas I was one of the rabble. So it was, at any rate; and often in the evening, returning from library or dining hall on the way to my distant Bœotia, I would drop in at his room, in a lofty corner of old Barclay Hall, to pick up note-books or anything else I might have left there.

What a pleasant place is a college dormitory at night! The rooms with their green-hooded lights and boyish similarity of decoration, the amiable buzz and stir of a game of cards under festoons of tobacco smoke, the wiry tinkle of a mandolin distantly heard, sudden clatter subsiding again into a general humming quiet, the happy sense of solitude in multitude, these are the partial ingredients of that feeling no alumnus ever forgets. In his pensive citadel, my friend J—— would be sitting, with his pipe (one of those new "class pipes" with inlaid silver numerals, which appear among every college generation toward Christmas time of freshman year). In his lap would be the large green volume ("British Poets of the Nineteenth Century," edited by Professor Curtis Hidden Page) which was the textbook of that sophomore course. He was reading Keats. And his eyes were those of one who has seen a new planet swim into his ken.

I don't know how many evenings we spent there together. Probably only a few. I don't recall just how we communed, or imparted to one another our juvenile speculations. But I plainly remember how he would sit beside his desk-lamp and chuckle over the Ode to a Nightingale. He was a quizzical and quickly humorous creature, and Keats's beauties seemed to fill him not with melancholy or anguish, but with a delighted prostration of laughter. The "wormy circumstance" of the Pot of Basil, the Indian Maid nursing her luxurious sorrow, the congealing Beadsman and the palsied beldame Angela—these and a thousand quaintnesses of phrase moved him to a gush of glorious mirth. It was not that he did not appreciate the poet, but the unearthly strangeness of it all, the delicate contradiction of laws and behaviours known to freshmen, tickled his keen wits and emotions until they brimmed into puzzled laughter. "Away! Away!" he would cry—

> For I will fly to thee,
> Not charioted by Bacchus and his pards,
> But on the viewless wings of Poesy,
> Though the dull brain perplexes and retards-

and he would shout with merriment. Beaded bubbles winking at the brim; Throbbing throats' long, long melodious moan; Curious conscience burrowing like a mole; Emprison her soft hand and let her rave; Men slugs and human serpentry; Bade her steep her hair in weird syrops; Poor weak palsy-stricken churchyard thing; Shut her pure sorrow-drops with glad exclaim—such lines were to him a constant and exhilarating excitement. In the very simplicity and unsophistication of his approach to the poet was a virgin naïveté of discernment that an Edinburgh Reviewer would rarely attain. Here, he dimly felt, was the great key

> To golden palaces, strange minstrelsy,
> . . . aye, to all the mazy world
> Of silvery enchantment.

And in line after line of Endymion, as we pored over them together, he found the clear happiness of a magic that dissolved everything into lightness and freedom. It is agreeable to remember this man, preparing to be a building contractor, who loved Keats because he made him laugh. I wonder if the critics have not too insistently persuaded us to read our poet in a black-edged mood? After all, his nickname was "Junkets."

So it was that I first, in any transcending sense, fell under the empire of a poet. Here was an endless fountain of immortal drink: here was a history potent to send a young mind from its bodily tenement. The pleasure was too personal to be completely shared; for

The Autogenesis of a Poet

the most part J—— and I read not together, but each
by each, he sitting in his morris chair by the desk,
I sprawled upon his couch, reading, very likely, different poems, but communicating, now and then, a
sudden discovery. Probably I exaggerate the subtlety
of our enjoyment, for it is hard to review the unself-
scrutinizing moods of freshmanhood. It would be
hard, too, to say which enthusiast had the greater enjoyment: he, because these glimpses through magic
casements made him merry; I, because they made me
sad. Outside, the snow sparkled in the pure winter
night; the long lance windows of the college library
shone yellow-panelled through the darkness, and there
would be the occasional interruption of light-hearted
classmates. How perfectly it all chimed into the mood
of St. Agnes' Eve! The opening door would bring a
gust of lively sound from down the corridor, a swelling
jingle of music, shouts from some humorous "rough-
house" (probably those sophomores on the floor
below)—

> The boisterous, midnight, festive clarion
> The kettle-drum, and far-heard clarionet
> Affray his ears, though but in dying tone—
> The hall-door shuts again, and all the noise is gone.

It did not take very long for J—— to work through
the fifty pages of Keats reprinted in Professor Hidden
Page's anthology; and then he, a lone and laughing
faun among that pack of stern sophomores—so flewed,
so sanded, out of the Spartan kind, crook-knee'd and

[13]

dewlapped like Thessalian bulls—sped away into
thickets of Landor, Tennyson, the Brownings. There
I, an unprivileged and unsuspected hanger-on, lost
their trail, returning to my own affairs. For some
reason—I don't know just why—I never "took" that
course in Nineteenth Century Poets, in the classroom
at any rate. But just as Mr. Chesterton, in his glorious little book, "The Victorian Age in Literature,"
asserts that the most important event in English history was the event that never happened at all (you
yourself may look up his explanation) so perhaps the
college course that meant most to me was the one
I never attended. What it meant to those sophomores
of the class of 1909 is another gentle speculation.
Three years later, when I was a senior, and those
sophomores had left college, another youth and myself
were idly prowling about a dormitory corridor where
some of those same sophomores had previously lodged.
An unsuspected cupboard appeared to us, and rum-
maging in it we found a pile of books left there, forgotten, by a member of that class. It was a Saturday
afternoon, and my companion and I had been wondering how we could raise enough cash to go to town
for dinner and a little harmless revel. To shove those
books into a suitcase and hasten to Philadelphia by
trolley was the obvious caper; and Leary's famous old
bookstore ransomed the volumes for enough money to
provide an excellent dinner at Lauber's, where, in those
days, the thirty-cent bottle of sour claret was considered the true, the blushful Hippocrene. But among
the volumes was a copy of Professor Page's anthology

which had been used by one of J——'s companions in
that poetry course. This seemed to me too precious
to part with, so I retained it; still have it; and have
occasionally studied the former owner's marginal
memoranda. At the head of The Eve of St. Agnes
he wrote: "Middle Ages. N. Italy. Guelph, Gui-
billine." At the beginning of Endymion he recorded:
"Keats tries to be spiritualized by love for celestials."
Against Sleep and Poetry: "Desultory. Genius in the
larval state." The Ode on a Grecian Urn, he noted:
"Crystallized philosophy of idealism. Embalmed an-
ticipation." The Ode on Melancholy: "Non-Gothic.
Not of intellect or disease. Emotions."

Darkling I listen to these faint echoes from a vanished lecture room, and ponder. Did J—— keep his
copy of the book, I wonder, and did he annotate it
with lively commentary of his own? He left college
at the end of our second year, and I have not seen or
heard from him these thirteen years. The last I knew
—six years ago—he was a contractor in an Ohio city;
and (is this not significant?) in a letter written then
to another classmate, recalling some waggishness of
our own sophomore days, he used the phrase "Like
Ruth among the alien corn."

In so far as one may see turning points in a tangle
of yarn, or count dewdrops on a morning cobweb, I
may say that a few evenings with my friend J—— were
the decisive vibration that moved one more minor poet
toward the privilege and penalty of Parnassus. One
cannot nicely decipher such fragile causes and effects.
It was a year later before the matter became serious

enough to enforce abandoning library copies of Keats and buying an edition of my own. And this, too, may have been not unconnected with the gracious influence of the other sex as exhibited in a neighbouring athenæum; and was accompanied by a gruesome spate of florid lyrics: some (happily) secret, and some exposed with needless hardihood in a college magazine. The world, which has looked leniently upon many poetical minorities, regards such frenzies with tolerant charity and forgetfulness. But the wretch concerned may be pardoned for looking back in a mood of lingering enlargement. As Sir Philip Sidney put it, "Self-love is better than any gilding to make that seem gorgeous wherein ourselves be parties."

There is a vast deal of nonsense written and uttered about poetry. In an age when verses are more noisily and fluently circulated than ever before, it might seem absurd to plead in the Muse's defence. Yet poetry and the things poets love are pitifully weak to-day. In essence, poetry is the love of life—not mere brutish tenacity of sensation, but a passion for all the honesties that make life free and generous and clean. For two thousand years poets have mocked and taunted the cruelties and follies of men, but to what purpose? Wordsworth said: "In spite of difference of soil and climate, of language and manners, of laws and customs, in spite of things silently gone out of mind, and things violently destroyed, the Poet binds together by passion and knowledge the vast empire of human society, as it is spread over the whole earth, and over all time."

The Autogenesis of a Poet

Sometimes it seems as though "things violently destroyed," and the people who destroy them, are too strong for the poets. Where, now, do we see any cohesive binding together of humanity? Are we nearer these things than when Wordsworth and Coleridge walked and talked on the Quantock Hills or on that immortal road "between Porlock and Linton"? Hardy writes "The Dynasts," Joseph Conrad writes his great preface to "The Nigger of the *Narcissus*," but do the destroyers hear them? Have you read again, since the War, Gulliver's "Voyage to the Houyhnhnms," or Herman Melville's "Moby Dick"? These men wrote, whether in verse or prose, in the true spirit of poets; and Swift's satire, which the text-book writers all tell you is so gross and savage as to suggest the author's approaching madness, seems tender and suave by comparison with what we know to-day.

Poetry is the log of man's fugitive castaway soul upon a doomed and derelict planet. The minds of all men plod the same rough roads of sense; and in spite of much knavery, all win at times "an ampler ether, a diviner air." The great poets, our masters, speak out of that clean freshness of perception. We hear their voices—

I there before thee, in the country that well thou knowest,
Already arrived am inhaling the odorous air.

So it is not vain, perhaps, to try clumsily to tell how this delicious uneasiness first captured the spirit of one

[17]

who, if not a poet, is at least a lover of poetry. Thus he first looked beyond the sunset; stood, if not on Parnassus, tiptoe upon a little hill. And overhead a great wind was blowing.

THE OLD RELIABLE

EXPRESS train stalled in a snowdrift," said one.
"The irascible old white-haired gentleman in the
Pullman smoker; the good-natured travelling salesman;
the wistful young widow in the day coach, with her six-
year-old blue-eyed little daughter. A coal-black Pullman porter who braves the shrieking gale to bring in a
tree from the copse along the track. Red-headed
brakeman (kiddies of his own at home), frostbitten
by standing all night between the couplings, holding
parts of broken steampipe together so the Pullman car
will keep warm. Young widow and her child, of
course, sleeping in the Pullman; white-haired old
gentleman vacates his berth in their favour. Good-

natured travelling salesman up all night, making cigar-
band decorations for the Tree, which is all ready in
the dining car in the morning——"

"Old English inn on a desolate moor," said another.
"Bright fire of coals in the coffee room, sporting prints,
yellow old newspaper cutting framed on the mantelpiece
describing gruesome murder committed in the house in
1760. Terrible night of storm—sleet tingling on the
panes; crimson curtains fluttering in the draught;
roads crusted with ice; savoury fumes of roast goose,
plum pudding, and brandy. Pretty chambermaid in
evident anxiety about something; guest tries to kiss her
in the corridor; she's too distrait to give the matter
proper attention. She has heard faint agonized cries
above the howling of the gale——"

"I like the sound of hymns," ventured a third.
"Frosty vestibule of fashionable church, rolling thun-
ders of the organ, fringes of icicles silvered by moonlight,
poor old Salvation Army Santa Claus shivering outside
and tinkling his pathetic little bell. Humane note:
those scarlet Christmas robes of the Army not nearly
as warm as they look. Hard-hearted vestryman,
member of old Knickerbocker family, always wears
white margins on his vest, suddenly touched by compassion, empties the collection plate into Santa's bucket.
Santa hurries off to the S. A. headquarters crying 'The
little ones will bless you for this.' Vestryman accused
of having pocketed the collection, dreadful scandal, too
proud to admit what he had done with it——"

The Old Reliable

"Christmas Eve in the Ambrose Channel," cried a fourth. "A blizzard blowing. The pilot boat, sheathed with ice, wallowing in the teeth of the blinding storm, beats her way up to the lee of the great liner. The pilot, suddenly taken ill, lies gasping on the sofa of the tiny cabin. Impossible for him to take the great liner into port; 2,000 passengers eager to get home for Christmas. But who is this gallant little figure darting up the rope ladder with fluttering skirts? The pilot's fourteen-year-old daughter. '*I* will take the *Nausea* to her berth! I've spent all my life in the Bay, and know every inch of the channel.' Rough quartermaster weeps as she takes the wheel from his hands. 'Be easy in your mind, Captain,' she says; 'but before the customs men come aboard tell me one thing—have you got that bottle of Scotch for my Daddy?'"

"Big New York department store," insisted the fifth. "Beautiful dark-haired salesgirl at the silk stocking counter. Her slender form trembles with fatigue, but she greets all customers with brave, sweet courtesy. Awful crush, every one buying silk stockings. Kindly floorwalker, sees she is overtaxed, suggests she leave early. Dark girl refuses; says she must be faithful to the Christmas spirit; moreover, she daren't face the evening battle on the subway. Handsome man comes to the counter to buy. Suddenly a scream, a thud, horrified outcries. Hold back the crowd! Call a physician! No good; handsome man, dead, murdered. Dark-haired girl, still holding the fatal hatpin, taken in custody, crying hysterically 'When he gave me his name, I couldn't help it. He's the one who has caused all the trouble!' Floorwalker reverently covers the body with a cloth, then looks at the name on the sales slip. 'Gosh,' he cries, aghast, 'it's Coles Phillips!'"

The gathering broke up, and the five men strolled out into the blazing August sunshine. The sultry glow of midsummer beat down upon them, but their thoughts were far away. They were five popular authors comparing notes on the stories they were writing for the Christmas magazines.

IN MEMORIAM
FRANCIS BARTON GUMMERE

I OFTEN wonder what inward pangs of laughter or despair he may have felt as he sat behind the old desk in Chase Hall and watched us file in, year after year! Callow, juvenile, ignorant, and cocksure—grotesquely confident of our own manly fulness of worldly *savoir*—an absurd rabble of youths, miserable flintheads indeed for such a steel! We were the most unpromising of all material for the scholar's eye; comfortable, untroubled middle-class lads most of us, to whom study was neither a privilege nor a passion, but only a sober and decent way of growing old enough to enter business.

We did not realize how accurately—and perhaps a trifle grimly—the strong, friendly face behind the desk was searching us and sizing us up. He knew us for what we were—a group of nice boys, too sleek, too cheerfully secure, to show the ambition of the true student. There was among us no specimen of the lean and dogged crusader of learning that kindles the eye of the master: no fanatical Scot, such as rejoices the Oxford or Cambridge don; no liquid-orbed and hawk-faced Hebrew with flushed cheek bones, such as sets the pace in the class-rooms of our large universities. No: we were a hopelessly mediocre, well-fed, satisfied, and characteristically Quakerish lot. As far as the battle for learning goes, we were pacifists—conscientious objectors.

It is doubtful whether any really great scholar ever gave the best years of his life to so meagrely equipped a succession of youngsters! I say this candidly, and it is well it should be said, for it makes apparent the true genius of Doctor Gummere's great gift. He turned this following of humble plodders into lovers and zealots of the great regions of English letters. There was something knightly about him—he, the great scholar, who would never stoop to scoff at the humblest of us. It might have been thought that his shining gifts were wasted in a small country college, where not one in fifty of his pupils could follow him into the enchanted lands of the imagination where he was fancy-free. But it was not so. One may meet man after man, old pupils of his, who have gone on into the homely drudging rounds of business, the law, journalism—men whose faces will light up with affection and remembrance when Doctor Gummere's name is mentioned. We may have forgotten much of our Chaucer, our Milton, our Ballads—though I am sure we have none of us forgotten the deep and thrilling vivacity of his voice reciting:

Francis Barton Gummere

O where hae ye been, Lord Randal, my son?
O where hae ye been, my handsome young man?
I hae been to the wild wood; mither, make my bed soon,
For I'm weary wi' hunting and fain wald lie doun.

But what we learned from him lay in the very charm
of his personality. It was a spell that no one in his
class-room could escape. It shone from his sparkling
eye; it spoke in his irresistible humour; it moved in
every line of that well-loved face, in his characteristic
gesture of leaning forward and tilting his head a little to
one side as he listened, patiently, to whatever juvenile
surmises we stammered to express. It was the true
learning of which his favourite Sir Philip Sidney said:

This purifying of wit, this enriching of memory,
enabling of judgment, and enlarging of conceit, which
commonly we call learning, under what name soever it
come forth or to what immediate end soever it be di-
rected, the final end is to lead and draw us to as high a
perfection as our degenerate souls, made worse by their
clay lodgings, can be capable of.

Indeed, just to listen to him was a purifying of wit, an
enriching of memory, an enabling of judgment, an enlarging of imagination. He gave us "so sweet a prospect into the way as will entice any man to enter into
it."

He moved among all human contacts with un-
erring grace. He was never the teacher, always
the comrade. It was his way to pretend that we
knew far more than we did; so with perfect courtesy and gravity, he would ask our opinion on some

matter of which we knew next to nothing; and we knew it was only his exquisiteness of good manners that impelled the habit; and we knew he knew the laughableness of it; yet we adored him for it. He always suited his strength to our weakness; would tell us things almost with an air of apology for seeming to know more than we; pretending that we doubtless had known it all along, but it had just slipped our memory. Marvellously he set us on our secret honour to do justice to this rare courtesy. To fail him in some task he had set became, in our boyish minds, the one thing most abhorrent in dealing with such a man—a discourtesy. He was a man of the rarest and most delicate breeding, the finest and truest gentleman we had known. Had he been nothing else, how much we would have learnt from that alone.

What a range, what a grasp, there was in his glowing, various mind! How open it was on all sides, how it teemed with interests, how different from the scholar of silly traditional belief! We used to believe that he could have taught us history, science, economics, philosophy —almost anything; and so indeed he did. He taught us to go adventuring among masterpieces on our own account, which is the most any teacher can do. Luckiest of all were those who, on one pretext or another, found their way to his fireside of an evening. To sit entranced, smoking one of his cigars,* to hear him talk of Stevenson, Meredith, or Hardy—(his favourites among the moderns) to marvel anew at the infinite

---

*It was characteristic of him that he usually smoked *Robin Hood*, that admirable 5-cent cigar, because the name, and the picture of an outlaw on the band, reminded him of the 14th century Ballads he knew by heart.

scope and vivacity of his learning—this was to live on the very doorsill of enchantment. Homeward we would go, crunching across the snow to where Barclay crowns the slope with her evening blaze of lights, one glimpse nearer some realization of the magical colours and tissues of the human mind, the rich perplexity and many-sided glamour of life.

It is strange (as one reviews all the memories of that good friend and master) to think that there is now a new generation beginning at Haverford that will never know his spell. There is a heavy debt on his old pupils. He made life so much richer and more interesting for us. Even if we never explored for ourselves the fields of literature toward which he pointed, his radiant individuality remains in our hearts as a true exemplar of what scholarship can mean. We can never tell all that he meant to us. Gropingly we turn to little pictures in memory. We see him crossing Cope Field in the green and gold of spring mornings, on his way to class. We see him sitting on the verandah steps of his home on sunny afternoons, full of gay and eager talk on a thousand diverse topics. He little knew, I think, how we hung upon his words. I can think of no more genuine tribute than this: that in my own class—which was a notoriously cynical and scoffish band of young sophisters—when any question of religious doubt or dogma arose for discussion among some midnight group, someone was sure to say, "I wish I knew what Doctor Gummere thought about it!" We felt instinctively that what he thought would have been convincing enough for us.

Plum Pudding

He was a truly great man. A greater man than we deserved, and there is a heavy burden upon us to justify the life that he gave to our little college. He has passed into the quiet and lovely tradition that surrounds and nourishes that place we all love so well. Little by little she grows, drawing strength and beauty from human lives around her, confirming herself in honour and remembrance. The teacher is justified by his scholars. Doctor Gummere might have gone elsewhere, surrounded by a greater and more ambitiously documented band of pupils. He whom we knew as the greatest man we had ever seen, moved little outside the world of learning. He gave himself to us, and we are the custodians of his memory.

Every man who loved our vanished friend must know with what realization of shamed incapacity one lays down the tributary pen. He was so strong, so full of laughter and grace, so truly a man, his long vacation still seems a dream, and we feel that somewhere on the well-beloved campus we shall meet him and feel that friendly hand. In thinking of him I am always reminded of that fine old poem of Sir Henry Wotton, a teacher himself, the provost of Eton, whose life has been so charmingly written by another Haverfordian— (Logan Pearsall Smith).

THE CHARACTER OF A HAPPY LIFE

How happy is he born and taught
  That serveth not another's will;
Whose armour is his honest thought,
  And simple truth his utmost skill!

Francis Barton Gummere

Whose passions not his masters are;
   Whose soul is still prepared for death
Not tied unto the world by care
   Of public fame or private breath;

Who envies none that chance doth raise,
   Nor vice; who never understood
How deepest wounds are given by praise;
   Nor rules of state, but rules of good;

Who hath his life from rumours freed;
   Whose conscience is his strong retreat;
Whose state can neither flatterers feed,
   Nor ruin make oppressors great;

Who God doth late and early pray
   More of His grace than gifts to lend;
And entertains the harmless day
   With a well-chosen book or friend;

This man is freed from servile bands
   Of hope to rise or fear to fall:
Lord of himself, though not of lands,
   And having nothing, yet hath all.

Such was the Happy Man as Sir Henry Wotton
described him. Such, I think, was the life of our friend.
I think it must have been a happy life, for he gave
so much happiness to others.

ADVENTURES AT LUNCH TIME

THIS window by which we sit is really very trying to our spirit.   On a clear fluid blue day the
sunlight pours over the cliffs and craggy coves and
angles of the great buildings round St. Paul's church-
yard.   We can see the temptation of being a cubist
painter as we study all those intersecting planes of light
and shadow.   Across the way, on Fulton Street, above
the girl in a green hat who is just now ingurgitating a
phial of orangeade, there are six different roof levels,
rising like steps toward the gold lightning bolts of the
statue on top of the Telephone and Telegraph Building.

Adventures at Lunch Time

Each of these planes carries its own particular impact of light or shadow. The sunshine seems to flow like an impalpable cataract over the top of the Hudson Terminal, breaking and shining in a hundred splashes and pools of brightness among the stone channels below. Far down the course of Church Street we can see the top floors of the Whitehall Building. We think of the little gilt ball that darts and dances so merrily in the fountain jet in front of that building. We think of the merry mercators of the Whitehall Club sitting at lunch on the cool summit of that great edifice. We think of the view as seen from there, the olive-coloured gleam of the water, the ships and tugs speckled about the harbour. And, looking down, we can see a peaceful gentleman sitting on a bench in St. Paul's graveyard, reading a book. We think seriously of writing a note, *"What are you reading?"* and weighting it with an inkwell and hurling it down to him. This window continually draws our mind outward and sets us speculating, when we ought to be answering letters or making inquiries of coal dealers as to whether there is any chance of getting a supply for next winter.

On such a day, having in mind that we ought to write another chapter of our book "How to Spend Three Hours at Lunch Time," we issued forth with Endymion to seek refreshment. It was a noontide to stir even the most carefully fettered bourgeois to impulses of escapade and foray. What should we do? At first we had some thought of showing to Endymion the delightful subterranean passage that leads from the

[31]

cathedral grottoes of the Woolworth Building to the City Hall subway station, but we decided we could not bear to leave the sunlight. So we chose a path at random and found ourselves at the corner of Beekman and Gold streets.

Now our intention was to make tracks toward Hanover Square and there to consider the world as viewed over the profile of a slab of cheesecake; but on viewing the agreeable old house at the corner of Gold Street— "The Old Beekman, Erected 1827," once called the Old Beekman Halfway House, but now the Old Beekman Luncheonette—no hungry man in his senses could pass without tarrying. A flavour of comely and respectable romance was apparent in this pleasant place, with its neat and tight-waisted white curtains in the upstairs windows and an outdoor stairway leading up to the second floor. Inside, at a table in a cool, dark corner, we dealt with hot dogs and cloudy cider in a manner beyond criticism. The name Luncheonette does this fine tavern serious injustice: there is nothing of the feminine or the soda fountain about it: it is robust, and we could see by the assured bearing of some well-satisfied habitués that it is an old landmark in that section.

But the brisk air and tempting serenity of the day made it seem emphatically an occasion for two lunches, and we passed on, along Pearl Street, in the bright checkerboard of sunbeams that slip through the trestles of the "L." It was cheerful to see that the same old Spanish cafés are still there, though we were a little disappointed to see that one of them has moved from its old-time quarters, where that fine brass-bound stairway led up from the street, to a new and gaudy palace on the other side. We also admired the famous and fascinating camp outfitting shop at 208 Pearl Street, which apparently calls itself WESTMINSTER ABBEY: but that is not the name of the shop but of the proprietor. We have been told that Mr. Abbey's father christened him so, intending him to enter the church. In the neighbourhood of Cliff and Pearl streets we browsed about enjoying the odd and savoury smells. There are all sorts of aromas in that part of the city, coffee and spices, drugs, leather, soap, and cigars. There was one very sweet, pervasive, and subtle smell, a caressing harmony for the nostril, which we pursued up and down various byways. Here it would quicken and grow almost strong enough for identification; then again it would become faint and hardly discernible. It had a rich, sweet oily tang, but we were at a loss to name it. We finally concluded that it was the bouquet of an "odourless disinfectant" that seemed to have its headquarters near by. In one place some bales of dried and withered roots were being loaded on a truck: they gave off a faint savour, which was familiar but baffling. On inquiry, these were sarsaparilla. Endymion was pleased with a sign on a doorway: "*Crude drugs and spices and essential oils.*" This, he said, was a perfect Miltonic line.

Hanover Square, however, was the apex of our pilgrimage. To come upon India House is like stepping back into the world of Charles Lamb. We had once lunched in the clubrooms upstairs with a charming

member and we had never forgotten the old seafaring
prints, the mustard pots of dark blue glass, the five-inch
mutton chops, the Victorian contour of the waiter's
waistcoat of green and yellow stripe. This time we
fared toward the tavern in the basement, where even
the outsider may penetrate, and were rejoiced by a
snug table in the corner. Here we felt at once the true
atmosphere of lunching, which is at its best when one
can get in a corner, next to some old woodwork rubbed
and shiny with age. Shandygaff, we found, was not
unknown to the servitor; and the cider that we saw
Endymion beaming upon was a blithe, clear yellow, as
merry to look at as a fine white wine. Very well, very
well indeed, we said to ourselves; let the world revolve;
in the meantime, what is that printed in blackface type
upon the menu? We have looked upon the faces of
many men, we have endured travail and toil and perplexity, we have written much rot and suffered much
inward shame to contemplate it; but in the meantime
(we said, gazing earnestly upon the face of Endymion),
in the meantime, we repeated, and before destiny
administers that final and condign chastisement that
we ripely merit, let us sit here in the corner of the India
House and be of good cheer. And at this point, matters
being so, and a second order of butter being already
necessary, the waiter arrived with the Spanish omelet.

Homeward by the way of South Street, admiring
the slender concave bows of fine ships—the *Mexico*
and the *Santa Marta*, for instance—and privily wondering what were our chances of smelling blue water
within the next quinquennium, we passed in mild and

placid abandonment. On Burling Slip, just where in former times there used to hang a sign KIPLING BREW (which always interested us), we saw a great, ragged, burly rogue sitting on a doorstep. He had the beard of a buccaneer, the placid face of one at ease with fortune. He hitched up his shirt and shifted from one ham to another with supreme and sunkissed contentment. And Endymion, who sees all things as the beginnings of heavenly poems, said merrily: "As I was walking on Burling Slip, I saw a seaman without a ship."

SECRET TRANSACTIONS OF THE THREE
HOURS FOR LUNCH CLUB

THE doctor having been elected a member of the club, a meeting was held to celebrate the event. Bowling Green, Esq., secretary, was instructed to prepare carefully confidential minutes. Weather: fair and tepid. Wind: N.N.E. Course laid: From starting line at a Church Street bookshop, where the doctor bought a copy of "Limbo," by Aldous Huxley, to Pier 56, N. R. Course made good: the same.

The doctor was in excellent form. On the Fourteenth Street car a human being was arguing fiercely and loudly with the conductor about some controversial

Secret Transactions

matter touching upon fares and destinations. The clamour was great. Said the doctor, adjusting his eyeglass and gazing with rebuke toward the disputants: "I will be gratified when this tumult subsides." The doctor has been added to the membership of the club in order to add social tone to the gathering. His charm is infinite; his manners are of a delicacy and an aplomb. His speech, when he is of waggish humour, carries a tincture of Queen Anne phraseology that is subtle and droll. A man, indeed! *L'extrême de charme*, as M. Djer-Kiss loves to say what time he woos the public in the theatre programmes.

The first thrill was when Bowling Green, Esq., secretary, cast an eye upward as the club descended from the Fourteenth Street sharabang, and saw, over the piers, the tall red funnels of the *Aquitania*. This is going to be great doings, said he to himself. O Cunard Line funnels! What is there that so moves the heart?

Bowling Green, Esq., confesses that it is hard to put these minutes into cold and calculated narrative. Among ships and seafaring concerns his heart is too violently stirred to be quite *maître de soi*.

The club moved forward. Welcomed by the suave commissionaire of the Cunard Line, it was invited to rise in the elevator. On the upper floor of the pier the members ran to the windows. There lay the *Aquitania* at her pier. The members' hearts were stirred. Even the doctor, himself a hardened man of the sea, showed a brilliant spark of emotion behind his monocular attic window. A ship in dock—and what a ship! A ship at a city pier, strange sight. It is like a lion in a circus cage. She, the beauty, the lovely living creature of open azure and great striding ranges of the sea, she that needs horizons and planets for her fitting perspective, she that asks the snow and silver at her irresistible stem, she that persecutes the sunset across the purple curves of the longitudes—tied up stiff and dead in the dull ditch of a dockway. The upward slope of that great bow, it was never made to stand still against a dusty pier-end.

The club proceeded and found itself in a little eddy of pure Scotland. The *Columbia* was just in from Glasgow—had docked only an hour before. The doctor became very Scots in a flash. "Aye, bonny!" was his reply to every question asked him by Mr. Green, the diligent secretary. The secretary was addressed as "lad." A hat now became a "bonnet." The fine stiff speech of Glasgow was heard on every side, for the passengers were streaming through the customs. Yon were twa bonny wee brithers, aiblins ten years old, that came marching off, with bare knees and ribbed woollen stockings and little tweed jackets. O Scotland, Scotland, said our hairt! The wund blaws snell frae the firth, whispered the secretary to himself, keeking about, but had not the courage to utter it.

Here the secretary pauses on a point of delicacy. It was the purpose of the club to visit Capt. David W. Bone of the *Columbia*, but the captain is a modest man, and one knows not just how much of our admiration of him and his ship he would care to see spread upon the minutes. Were Mr. Green such a man as the captain, would he be lowering himself to have any

truck with journalists and such petty folk? Mr. Green
would not. Mark you: Captain Bone is the master of an
Atlantic liner, a veteran of the submarine-haunted lanes
of sea, a writer of fine books (have you, lovers of sea
tales, read "The Brassbounder" and "Broken Stowage"?) a collector of first editions, a man who stood on
the bridge of the flagship at Harwich and watched the
self-defiled U-boats slink in and come to a halt at the
international code signal MN (Stop instantly!)—"Ha,"
said Mr. Green, "Were I such a man, I would pass by
like shoddy such pitifuls as colyumists." But he was a
glad man no less, for he knew the captain was bigger of
heart. Besides, he counted on the exquisite tact of the
doctor to see him through. Indeed, even the stern offi-
cials of the customs had marked the doctor as a man
exceptional. And as the club stood patiently among
the outward flux of authentic Glasgow, came the captain himself and welcomed them aboard.

Across immaculate decks, and in the immortal
whiff, indefinable, of a fine ship just off the high seas,
trod the beatified club. A ship, the last abiding place
in a mannerless world of good old-fashioned caste,
and respect paid upward with due etiquette and discipline through the grades of rank. The club, for a moment, were guests of the captain; deference was paid to
them. They stood in the captain's cabin (sacred
words). "Boy!" cried the captain, in tones of command. Not as one speaks to office boys in a newspaper kennel, in a voice of entreaty. The boy appeared: a curly-headed, respectful stripling. A look
of respect: how well it sits upon youth. "Boy!" said

the captain—but just what the captain said is not to be put upon vulgar minutes. Remember, pray, the club was upon British soil.

In the saloon sat the club, and their faces were the faces of men at peace, men harmonious and of delicate cheer. The doctor, a seafaring man, talked the lingo of imperial mariners: he knew the right things to say: he carried along the humble secretary, who gazed in melodious mood upon the jar of pickled onions. At sea Mr. Green is of lurking manners: he holds fast to his bunk lest worse befall; but a ship in port is his empire. Scotch broth was before them—pukka Scotch broth, the doctor called it; and also the captain and the doctor had some East Indian name for the chutney. The secretary resolved to travel and see the world. Curried chicken and rice was the word: and, not to exult too cruelly upon you (O excellent friends!), let us move swiftly over the gooseberry tart. There was the gooseberry tart, and again, a few minutes later, it was not there. All things have their appointed end. "Boy!" said the captain. (Must I remind you, we were on imperial soil.) Is it to be said that the club rose to the captain's cabin once more, and matters of admirable purport were tastefully discussed, as is the habit of us mariners?

"The drastic sanity of the sea"—it is a phrase from a review of one of the captain's own books, "Merchantmen-at-Arms," which this club (so it runs upon the minutes), as lovers of sea literature, officially hope may soon be issued on this side also. It is a phrase, if these minutes are correct, from a review written by H. M. Tomlinson, another writer of the sea, of whom we have spoken before, and may, in God's providence, again. "The drastic sanity of the sea" was the phrase that lingered in our mind as we heard the captain talk of books and of discipline at sea and of the trials imposed upon shipmasters by the La Follette act. (What, the club wondered inwardly, does Mr. La Follette know of seafaring?) "The drastic sanity of the sea!" We thought of other sailors we had known, and how they had found happiness and simplicity in the ordered combat with their friendly enemy. A virtue goes out of a ship (Joseph Conrad said, in effect) when she touches her quay. Her beauty and purpose are, for the moment, dulled and dimmed. But even there, how much she brings us. How much, even though we do not put it into words, the faces and accents of our seafaring friends give us in the way of plain wisdom and idealism. And the secretary, as he stepped aboard the hubbub of a subway train, was still pondering "the drastic sanity of the sea."

INITIATION

ALLURED by the published transactions of the club, our friend Lawton presented himself at the headquarters toward lunch time and announced himself as a candidate for membership. An executive session was hastily convened. Endymion broke the news to the candidate that initiates in this select organization are expected to entertain the club at luncheon. To the surprise of the club, our genial visitor neither shrank nor quailed. His face was bland and his bearing ambitious in the extreme. Very well, he said; as long as it isn't the Beaux Arts café.

The itinerary of the club for this day had already been arranged by the secretary. The two charter members, plus the high-spirited acolyte, made their way along West Street toward the Cortlandt Street ferry. It was plain from the outset that fortune had favoured

the organization with a new member of the most
sparkling quality. Every few yards a gallant witti-
cism fell from him. Some of these the two others
were able to juggle and return, but many were too flashing for them to cope with. In front of the ferry house
lay a deep and quaggish puddle of slime, crossable only
by ginger-footed work upon sheets of tin. Endymion
rafted his tenuous form across with a delicate straddle
of spidery limbs. The secretary followed, with a more
solid squashing technique. "Ha," cried the new member; "grace before meat!" Endymion and the secretary
exchanged secret glances. Lawton, although he knew
it not, was elected from that moment.

The ritual of the club, while stern toward initiates,
is not brutal. Since you are bursar for the lunch,
said the secretary, I will buy the ferry tickets, and he
did so. On the boat these carefree men gazed blithely
upon the shipping. "Little did I think," said Lawton,
"that I was going for a sea voyage." "That," said the
club, "is the kind of fellows we are. Whimsical. As
soon as we think of a thing, we don't do it."

"Is that the *Leviathan* up there?" said one of the
members, pointing toward a gray hull on the Hoboken
horizon. No one knew, but the secretary was reminded
of an adventure during the war. "One time I was
crossing on this ferry," he said, "and the *Leviathan*
passed right by us. It was just at dusk and her cam-
ouflage was wonderful. Her blotches and stripes were
so arranged that from a little distance, in the twilight,
she gave the impression of a much smaller vessel,
going the other way. All her upper works seemed to

fade out in the haze and she became a much smaller ship." "That would be a wonderful plan for some of these copious dowagers one sees," said the irreverent Lawton. "Yes," we said; "instead of a stout lady going in to dinner, you would see a slim flapper coming out."

Something was then said about a good friend of the club who had at one time worked for the Y. M. C. A. "What is he doing now?" asked one. "He's with Grace and Company," said the secretary. The candidate was unabashed. "Think," he said, "of a Y. M. C. A. man getting grace at last."

The club found the Jersey City terminal much as usual, and to our surprise the candidate kept up his courage nobly as he was steered toward the place of penance, being the station lunch counter. The club remembered this as a place of excellent food in days gone by, when trains from Philadelphia stopped here instead of at the Penn. Station. Placing the host carefully in the middle, the three sat down at the curving marble slab. The waiters immediately sensed that something unusual was toward. Two dashed up with courteous attentions. It was surmised by the club that the trio had happened to sit at a spot where the jurisdictions of two waiters met. Both the wings of the trio waved the waiters toward the blushing novice, making it plain that upon him lay all responsibility. "It is obvious," remarked the secretary, "that you, Lawton, are right on the boundary line where two waiters meet. You will have to tip them both."

The new member was game. "Well," he said, with-

out a trace of nervousness; "what'll you have?" The
choice fell upon breast of lamb. The secretary asked
for iced tea. Endymion, more ruthless, ordered ginger
ale. When the ginger ale came, Lawton, still waggish,
observed the label, which was one of the many imitations
of a well-known brand. "The man who invented the
diamond-shaped label," said Lawton, "was certainly a
pathfinder in the wilderness of the ginger ale business.
This ginger ale," said Lawton, tasting it, "is carefully
warmed, like old claret."

The club sought to keep their host's mind off the
painful topic of viands. "Sitting here makes one
feel as though he ought to be going to take a train somewhere," said one. "Yes, the express for Weehawken,"
said the vivacious host. From this it was only a step to
speaking of Brooklyn. The secretary explained that
the club had outlined a careful itinerary in that borough for proximate pursuit. Lawton told that he
had at one time written an essay on the effect of Brooklyn on the dialogue of the American drama. "It is the
butt end of Long Island," he cried, with cruel mirth.
Lovers of Brooklyn in the club nearly blackballed him
for this.

With ice cream and cottage pudding, the admirable
menu proceeded. The waiters conferred secretly together. They carefully noted the cheerful carving of
the host's brow. They will know him again. A man
who bursts in suddenly upon a railroad lunch counter
and pays for three such meals, here is an event in the
grim routine! But perhaps the two charter members
were feeling pangs of conscience. "Come," they said,

"at least let us split the ginger ale checks." But Lawton was seeing it through. Not a drum was heard, not a funeral note, as our host to the cashier we hurried. The secretary bought a penny box of matches and lit the great man's cigarette for him. Endymion, equally stirred, ran to buy the ferry tickets for the return voyage. "This time," he said, "I will be the ferry godmother."

On the homeward passage a little drowse fell upon the two charter members. They had lunched more richly than was their wont. "Oh, these distressing, heavy lunches!" as Aldous Huxley cries in one of his poems. But Lawton was still of bright vivacity. At that time the club was perturbed by the coming Harding-Cox election. "Which of the vice-presidents are you going to vote for?" he cried, and then said: "It looks to me like Debs or dubs."

Endymion and the secretary looked at each other solemnly. The time had come. "I, Endymion," said the chairman, "take thee, Lawton, to have and to hold, as a member of the club."

And the secretary tenderly pronounced the society's formula for such occasions: "There is no inanition in an initiation."

CREED OF THE THREE HOURS FOR LUNCH CLUB

IT HAS been suggested that the Three Hours for Lunch Club is an immoral institution; that it is founded upon an insufficient respect for the devotions of industry; that it runs counter to the form and pressure of the age; that it encourages a greedy and rambling humour in the young of both sexes; that it even punctures, in the bosoms of settled merchants and rotarians, that capsule of efficiency and determination by which Great Matters are Put Over. It has been said, in short, that the Three Hours for Lunch Club should be more clandestine and reticent about its truancies.

Accordingly, it seems good to us to testify concerning Lunches and the philosophy of Lunching.

There are Lunches of many kinds. The Club has

Plum Pudding

been privileged to attend gatherings of considerable
lustre; occasions when dishes of richness and curiosity
were dissected; when the surroundings were not devoid of glamour and surreptitious pomp. The Club
has been convened in many different places: in resorts of
pride and in low-ceiled reeky taphouses; in hotels where
those clear cubes of unprofitable ice knock tinklingly in
the goblets; in the brightly tinted cellars of Greenwich
Village; in the saloons of ships. But the Club would
give a false impression of its mind and heart if it allowed any one to suppose that Food is the chief object
of its quest. It is true that Man, bitterly examined,
is merely a vehicle for units of nourishing combustion;
but on those occasions when the Club feels most truly
Itself it rises above such considerations.

The form and pressure of the time (to repeat Ham-
let's phrase) is such that thoughtful men—and of such
the Club is exclusively composed: men of great heart,
men of nice susceptibility—are continually oppressed
by the fumbling, hasty, and insignificant manner in
which human contacts are accomplished. Let us even
say, *masculine* contacts: for the first task of any philosopher being to simplify his problem so that he can examine it clearly and with less distraction, the Club
makes a great and drastic purge by sweeping away
altogether the enigmatic and frivolous sex and disre-
garding it, at any rate during the hours of convivial
session. The Club is troubled to note that in the in-
tolerable rabies and confusion of this business life
men meet merely in a kind of convulsion or horrid
passion of haste and perplexity. We see, ever and

often, those in whose faces we discern delightful and considerable secrets, messages of just import, grotesque mirth, or improving sadness. In their bearing and gesture, even in hours of haste and irritation, the Club (with its trained and observant eye) notes the secret and rare sign of Thought. Such men are marked by an inexorable follow-up system. Sooner or later their telephones ring; secretaries and go-betweens are brushed aside; they are bidden to appear at such and such a time and place; no excuses are accepted. Then follow the Consolations of Intercourse. Conducted with "shattering candour" (as one has said who is in spirit a member of this Club, though not yet, alas, inducted), the meetings may sometimes resolve themselves into a ribaldry, sometimes into a truthful pursuit of Beauty, sometimes into a mere logomachy. But in these symposiums, unmarred by the crude claim of duty, the Club does with single-minded resolve pursue the only lasting satisfaction allowed to humanity, to wit, the sympathetic study of other men's minds.

This is clumsily said: but we have seen moments when eager and honourable faces round the board explained to us what we mean. There is but one indefeasible duty of man, to say out the truth that is in his heart. The way of life engendered by a great city and a modern civilization makes it hard to do so. It is the function of the Club to say to the City and to Life Itself: "Stand back! Fair play! We see a goodly matter inditing in our friend's spirit. We will take our ease and find out what it is."

For this life of ours (asserts the Club) is curiously

compounded of Beauty and Dross. You ascend the Woolworth Building, let us say—one of man's noblest and most poetic achievements. And at the top, what do you find, just before going out upon that gallery to spread your eye upon man's reticulated concerns? Do you find a little temple or cloister for meditation, or any way of marking in your mind the beauty and significance of the place? No, a man in uniform will thrust into your hand a booklet of well-intentioned description (but of unapproachable typographic ugliness) and you will find before you a stall for the sale of cheap souvenirs, ash trays, and hideous postcards. In such ways do things of Beauty pass into the custody of those unequipped to understand them.

The Club thinks that the life of this city, brutally intense and bewildering, has yet a beauty and glamour and a secret word to the mind, so subtle that it cannot be closely phrased, but so important that to miss it is to miss life itself. And to forfeit an attempt to see, understand, and mutually communicate this loveliness is to forfeit that burning spark that makes men's spirits worth while. To such halting meditations the Club devotes its aspirations undistressed by humorous protest. If this be treason. . . !

A PREFACE TO THE PROFESSION OF JOURNALISM

(BEING AN ANSWER TO A LETTER FROM A COLLEGE STUDENT, ASKING ADVICE AS TO TAKING UP WRITING AS A CAREER)

YOUR inquiry is congenial, and I feel guilty of selfishness in answering it in this way. But he must be a poor workman, whether artisan or artist, who does not welcome an excuse now and then for shutting out the fascinating and maddening complexity of this shining world to concentrate his random wits on some honest and self-stimulating expression of his purpose.

There are exceptions to every rule; but writing, if undertaken as a trade, is subject to the conditions of all other trades. The apprentice must begin with task-work; he must please his employers before he can earn the right to please himself. Not only that, he must have ingenuity and patience enough to learn *how* editors are pleased; but he will be startled, I think, if he studies their needs, to see how eager they are to meet him half way. This necessary docility is in the long run, a wholesome physic, because, if our apprentice has any gallantry of spirit, it will arouse in him an exhilarating irritation, that indignation which is said to be the forerunner of creation. It will mean, probably, a period—perhaps short, perhaps long, perhaps permanent—of rather meagre and stinted acquaintance with the genial luxuries and amenities of life; but (such is the optimism of memory) a period that he will always look back upon as the happiest of all. It is well for our apprentice if, in this season, he has a taste for cheap tobacco and a tactful technique in borrowing money.

The deliberate embrace of literature as a career involves very real dangers. I mean dangers to the spirit over and above those of the right-hand trouser pocket. For, let it be honestly stated, the business of writing is solidly founded on a monstrous and perilous egotism. Himself, his temperament, his powers of observation and comment, his emotions and sensibilities and ambitions and idiocies—these are the only monopoly the writer has. This is his only capital, and with glorious and shameless confidence he proposes to market it. Let him make the best of it. Continually stooping over the muddy flux of his racing mind, searching a momentary flash of clearness in which he can find mirrored some delicate beauty or truth, he tosses be-

A Preface to the Profession

tween the alternatives of self-grandeur and self-disgust. It is a painful matter, this endless self-scrutiny. We are all familiar with the addled ego of literature—the writer whom constant self-communion has made vulgar, acid, querulous, and vain. And yet it is remarkable that of so many who meddle with the combustible passions of their own minds so few are blown up. The discipline of living is a fine cooling-jacket for the engine.

It is essential for our apprentice to remember that, though he begin with the vilest hack-work—writing scoffing paragraphs, or advertising pamphlets, or free-lance snippets for the papers—that even in hack-work quality shows itself to those competent to judge; and he need not always subdue his gold to the lead in which he works. Moreover, conscience and instinct are surprisingly true and sane. If he follows the suggestions of his own inward, he will generally be right. Moreover again, no one can help him as much as he can help himself. There is no job in the writing world that he cannot have if he really wants it. Writing about something he intimately knows is a sound principle. Hugh Walpole, that greatly gifted novelist, taught school after leaving Cambridge, and very sensibly began by writing about school-teaching. If you care to see how well he did it, read "The Gods and Mr. Perrin." I would propose this test to the would-be writer: Does he feel, honestly, that he could write as convincingly about his own tract of life (whatever it may be) as Walpole wrote about that boys' school? If so, he has a true vocation for literature.

Plum Pudding

The first and most necessary equipment of any writer, be he reporter, advertising copy-man, poet, or historian, is swift, lively, accurate observation. And since consciousness is a rapid, shallow river which we can only rarely dam up deep enough to go swimming and take our ease, it is his positive need (unless he is a genius who can afford to let drift away much of his only source of gold) to keep a note-book handy for the sieving and skimming of this running stream. Samuel Butler has good advice on this topic. Of ideas, he says, you must throw salt on their tails or they fly away and you never see their bright plumage again. Poems, stories, epigrams, all the happiest freaks of the mind, flit by on wings and at haphazard instants. They must be caught in air. In this respect one thinks American writers ought to have an advantage over English, for American trousers are made with hip-pockets, in which a small note-book may so comfortably caress the natural curvature of man.

Fancy is engendered in the eyes, said Shakespeare, and is with gazing fed. By fancy he meant (I suppose) love; but imagination is also so engendered. Close, constant, vivid, and compassionate gazing at the ways of mankind is the laboratory manual of literature. But for most of us we may gaze until our eyeballs twitch with weariness; unless we seize and hold the flying picture in some steadfast memorandum, the greater part of our experience dissolves away with time. If a man has thought sufficiently about the arduous and variously rewarded profession of literature to propose seriously to follow it for a living, he will already

[54]

A Preface to the Profession

have said these things to himself, with more force and
pungency. He may have satisfied himself that he has
a necessary desire for "self-expression," which is a
parlous state indeed, and the cause of much literary
villainy. The truly great writer is more likely to write
in the hope of expressing the hearts of others than his
own. And there are other desires, too, most legitimate,
that he may feel. An English humorist said recently
in the preface to his book: "I wrote these stories to
satisfy an inward craving—not for artistic expression,
but for food and drink." But I cannot conscientiously
advise any man to turn to writing merely as a means of
earning his victual unless he should, by some cheerful
casualty, stumble upon a trick of the You-know-me-
Alfred sort, what one might call the Attabuoyant
style. If all you want is a suggestion as to some
honest way of growing rich, the doughnut industry is
not yet overcrowded; and people will stand in line
to pay twenty-two cents for a dab of ice-cream smeared
with a trickle of syrup.

To the man who approaches writing with some decent
tincture of idealism it is well to say that he proposes to
use as a trade what is, at its best and happiest, an art
and a recreation. He proposes to sell his mental reactions to the helpless public, and he proposes not only
to enjoy himself by so doing, but to be handsomely
recompensed withal. He cannot complain that in days
when both honesty and delicacy of mind are none too
common we ask him to bring to his task the humility of
the tradesman, the joy of the sportsman, the conscience
of the artist.

And if he does so, he will be in a condition to profit by these fine words of George Santayana, said of the poet, but applicable to workers in every branch of literature:

"He labours with his nameless burden of perception, and wastes himself in aimless impulses of emotion and reverie, until finally the method of some art offers a vent to his inspiration, or to such part of it as can survive the test of time and the discipline of expression. . . . Wealth of sensation and freedom of fancy, which make an extraordinary ferment in his ignorant heart, presently bubble over into some kind of utterance."

FULTON STREET, AND WALT WHITMAN

AT THE suggestion of Mr. Christopher Clarke, the
Three Hours for Lunch Club made pilgrimage to
the old seafaring tavern at No. 2 Fulton Street, and
found it to be a heavenly place, with listing brass-shod
black walnut stairs and the equally black and delightful
waiter called Oliver, who (said Mr. Clarke) has been
there since 1878.

But the club reports that the swordfish steak, of
which it partook as per Mr. Clarke's suggestion, did not
appeal so strongly to its taste. Swordfish steak, we
feel, is probably a taste acquired by long and diligent
application. At the first trial it seemed to the club a
bit too reptilian in flavour. The club will go there
again, and will hope to arrive in time to grab one of
those tables by the windows, looking out over the
docks and the United Fruit Company steamer which is
so appropriately named the *Banan;* but it is the sense
of the meeting that swordfish steak is not in its line.

Plum Pudding

The club retorts to Mr. Clarke by asking him if he knows the downtown chophouse where one may climb sawdusted stairs and sit in a corner beside a framed copy of the *New-York Daily Gazette* of May 1, 1789, at a little table incised with the initials of former habitués, and hold up toward the light a glass of the clearest and most golden and amberlucent cider known to mankind, and before attacking a platter of cold ham and Boston beans, may feel that smiling sensation of a man about to make gradual and decent advances toward a ripe and ruddy appetite.

Fulton Street has always been renowned for its taverns. The Old Shakespeare Tavern used to be there, as is shown by the tablet at No. 136 commemorating the foundation of the Seventh Regiment. The club has always intended to make more careful exploration of Dutch Street, the little alley that runs off Fulton Street on the south side, not far from Broadway. There is an eating place on this byway, and the organization plans to patronize it, in order to have an excuse for giving itself the sub-title of the Dutch Street Club. The more famous eating houses along Fulton Street are known to all: the name of at least one of them has a genial Queen Anne sound. And only lately a very seemly coffee house was established not far from Fulton and Nassau. We must confess our pleasure in the fact that this place uses as its motto a footnote from The *Spectator*—"Whoever wished to find a gentleman commonly asked not where he resided, but which coffee house he frequented."

Among the many things to admire along Fulton

Fulton Street, and Walt Whitman

Street (not the least of which are Dewey's puzzling per·
petually fluent grape-juice bottle, and the shop where
the trained ferrets are kept, for chasing out rats, mice,
and cockroaches from your house, the sign says) we vote
for that view of the old houses along the south side of the
street, where it widens out toward the East River.
This vista of tall, leaning chimneys seems to us one of
the most agreeable things in New York, and we wonder
whether any artist has ever drawn it. As our colleague
Endymion suggested, it would make a fine subject for
Walter Jack Duncan. In the eastern end of this strip
of fine old masonry resides the seafaring tavern we
spoke of above; formerly known as Sweet's, and a
great place of resort (we are told) for Brooklynites in
the palmy days before the Bridge was opened, when
they used to stop there for supper before taking the
Fulton Ferry across the perilous tideway.

The Fulton Ferry—dingy and deserted now—is full
of fine memories. The old waiting room, with its or-
nate carved ceiling and fine, massive gas brackets,
peoples itself, in one's imagination, with the lively and
busy throngs of fifty and sixty years ago. "My life
then (1850-60) was curiously identified with Fulton
Ferry, already becoming the greatest in the world for
general importance, volume, variety, rapidity, and
picturesqueness." So said Walt Whitman. It is a
curious experience to step aboard one of the boats in the
drowsy heat of a summer afternoon and take the short
voyage over to the Brooklyn slip, underneath one of the
huge piers of the Bridge. A few heavy wagons and
heat-oppressed horses are almost the only other passen-

gers. Not far away from the ferry, on the Brooklyn side, are the three charmingly named streets—Cranberry, Orange, and Pineapple—which are also so lastingly associated with Walt Whitman's life. It strikes us as odd, incidentally, that Walt, who loved Brooklyn so much, should have written a phrase so capable of humorous interpretation as the following: "Human appearances and manners—endless humanity in all its phases—Brooklyn also." This you will find in Walt's Prose Works, which is (we suppose) one of the most neglected of American classics.

But Fulton Street, Manhattan—in spite of its two greatest triumphs: Evelyn Longman Batchelder's glorious figure of "Lightning," and the strictly legal "three grains of pepsin" which have been a comfort to so many stricken invalids—is a mere byway compared to Fulton Street, Brooklyn, whose long bustling channel may be followed right out into the Long Island pampas. At the corner of Fulton and Cranberry streets "Leaves of Grass" was set up and printed, Walt Whitman himself setting a good deal of the type. Ninety-eight Cranberry Street, we have always been told, was the address of Andrew and James Rome, the printers. The house at that corner is still numbered 98. The ground floor is occupied by a clothing store, a fruit stand, and a barber shop. The building looks as though it is probably the same one that Walt knew. Opposite it is a sign

Fulton Street, and Walt Whitman

where the comparatively innocent legend BEN'S PURE LAGER has been deleted.

The pilgrim on Fulton Street will also want to have a look at the office of the Brooklyn *Eagle*, that famous paper which has numbered among its employees two such different journalists as Walt Whitman and Edward Bok. There are many interesting considerations to be drawn from the two volumes of Walt's writings for the *Eagle*, which were collected (under the odd title "The Gathering of the Forces") by Cleveland Rodgers and John Black. We have always been struck by the complacent naïveté of Walt's judgments on literature(written, perhaps, when he was in a hurry to go swimming down at the foot of Fulton Street). Such remarks as the following make us ponder a little sadly. Walt wrote:

We are no admirer of such characters as Doctor Johnson. He was a sour, malicious, egotistical man. He was a sycophant of power and rank, withal; his biographer narrates that he "always spoke with rough contempt of popular liberty." His head was educated to the point of *plus*, but for his heart, might still more unquestionably stand the sign *minus*. He insulted his equals . . . and tyrannized over his inferiors. He fawned upon his superiors, and, of course, loved to be fawned upon himself. . . . Nor were the freaks of this man the mere "eccentricities of genius"; they were probably the faults of a vile, low nature. His soul was a bad one.

The only possible comment on all this is that it is absurd, and that evidently Walt knew very little about the great Doctor. One of the curious things about Walt —and there is no man living who admires him more

Plum Pudding

than we do—is that he requires to be forgiven more generously than any other great writer. There is no one who has ever done more grotesquely unpardonable things than he—and yet, such is the virtue of his great, saline simplicity, one always pardons them. As a book reviewer, to judge from the specimens rescued from the *Eagle* files by his latest editors, he was uniquely childish.

Noting the date of Walt's blast on Doctor Johnson (December 7, 1846), it is doubtful whether we can attribute the irresponsibility of his remarks to a desire to go swimming.

The editors of this collection venture the suggestion that the lighter pieces included show Walt as "not devoid of humour." We fear that Walt's waggishness was rather heavily shod. Here is a sample of his light-hearted paragraphing (the italics are his):—

Carelessly knocking a man's eye out with a broken axe, may be termed a *bad axe-i-dent.*

It was in Leon Bazalgette's "Walt Whitman" that we learned of Walt's only really humorous achievement; and even then the humour was unconscious. It seems that during the first days of his life as a journalist in New York, Walt essayed to compromise with Manna-hatta by wearing a frock coat, a high hat, and a flower in his lapel. We regret greatly that no photo of Walt in this rig has been preserved, for we would like to have seen the gentle misery of his bearing.

McSORLEY'S

THIS afternoon we have been thinking how pleasant it would be to sit at one of those cool tables up at McSorley's and write our copy there. We have always been greatly allured by Dick Steele's habit of writing his Tatler at his favourite tavern. You remember his announcement, dated April 12, 1709:

All accounts of gallantry, pleasure, and entertainment, shall be under the article of White's Chocolate-house; poetry, under that of Will's Coffee-house; learning, under the title of The Grecian; foreign and domestic news, you will have from Saint James's Coffee-house; and what else I have to offer on any other subject shall be dated from my own apartment.

Sir Dick—would one speak of him as the first colyumist?—continued by making what is, we suppose,

[63]

one of the earliest references in literature to the newspaper man's "expense account." But the expenses of
the reporter two centuries ago seem rather modest.
Steele said:

I once more desire my reader to consider that as I
cannot keep an ingenious man to go daily to Will's
under twopence each day, merely for his charges; to
White's under sixpence; nor to The Grecian, without
allowing him some plain Spanish, to be as able as others
at the learned table; and that a good observer cannot
speak with even Kidney* at Saint James's without
clean linen: I say, these considerations will, I hope,
make all persons willing to comply with my humble
request of a penny-a-piece.

But what we started to say was that if, like Dick
Steele, we were in the habit of dating our stuff from
various inns around the town, our choice for a quiet
place in which to compose items of "gallantry, pleasure,
and entertainment" would be McSorley's—"The Old
House at Home"—up on Seventh Street. We had
feared that this famous old cabin of cheer might have
gone west in the recent evaporation; but rambling
round in the neighbourhood of the Cooper Union we
saw its familiar doorway with a shock of glad surprise.
After all, there is no reason why the old-established
houses should not go on doing a good business on a
Volstead basis. It has never been so much a question
of what a man drinks as the atmosphere in which he
drinks it. Atrocious cleanliness and glitter and raw
naked marble make the soda fountains a disheartening

---

* Evidently the bus boy.

place to the average male. He likes a dark, low-ceil-
inged, and not too obtrusively sanitary place to take
his ease. At McSorley's is everything that the innocent
fugitive from the world requires. The great amiable
cats that purr in the back room. The old pictures
and playbills on the walls. The ancient clocks that
hoarsely twang the hours. We cannot imagine a happier place to sit down with a pad of paper and a well-
sharpened pencil than at that table in the corner by the
window. Or the table just under that really lovely
little portrait of Robert Burns—would there be any
more propitious place in New York at which to fashion
verses? There would be no interruptions, such as make
versifying almost impossible in a newspaper office.
The friendly bartenders in their lilac-coloured shirts are
wise and gracious men. They would not break in upon
one's broodings. Every now and then, while the hot
sun smote the awnings outside, there would be another
china mug of that one-half-of-1-per-cent. ale, which
seems to us very good. We repeat: we don't care so
much what we drink as the surroundings among which
we drink it. We are not, if you will permit the phrase,
sot in our ways. We like the spirit of McSorley's,
which is decent, dignified, and refined. No club has an
etiquette more properly self-respecting.

One does not go to McSorley's without a glimpse at
that curious old red pile Bible House. It happened this
way: Our friend Endymion was back from his vacation
and we were trying to celebrate it in modest fashion.
We were telling him all the things that had happened
since he went away—that Bob Holliday had had a for-

tieth birthday, and Frank Shay had published his
bibliography of Walt Whitman, and all that sort of
thing; and in our mutual excitement Endymion whisked
too swiftly round a corner and caught his jacket on a
sharp door-latch and tore it. Inquiring at Astor
Place's biggest department store as to where we could
get it mended, they told us to go to "Mr. Wright the
weaver" on the sixth floor of Bible House, and we did
so. On our way back, avoiding the ancient wire rope
elevator (we know only one other lift so delightfully
mid-Victorian, viz., one in Boston, that takes you upstairs to see Edwin Edgett, the gentle-hearted literary
editor of the Boston *Transcript*), we walked down the
stairs, peeping into doorways in great curiosity. The
whole building breathed a dusky and serene quaintness
that pricks the imagination. It is a bit like the shop
in Edinburgh (on the corner of the Leith Walk and An-
tigua Street, if we remember) that R. L. S. described
in "A Penny Plain and Twopence Coloured"—"it
was dark and smelt of Bibles." We looked in at the
entrance to the offices of the *Christian Herald*. The
Bowling Green thought that what he saw was two
young ladies in close and animated converse; but
Endymion insisted that it was one young lady doing
her hair in front of a large mirror. "Quite a pretty
little picture," said Endymion. We argued about this
as we went down the stairs. Finally we went back
to make sure. Endymion was right. Even in the
darkness of Bible House, we agreed, romance holds
sway. And then we found a book shop on the ground
floor of Bible House. One of our discoveries there was

McSorley's

"Little Mr. Bouncer," by Cuthbert Bede—a companion volume to "Mr. Verdant Green."

But Dick Steele's idea of writing his column from different taverns round the city is rather gaining ground in our affections. There would be no more exciting way of spending a fortnight or so than in taking a walking tour through the forests of New York, camping for the night wherever we happened to find ourself at dark, Adam-and-Evesdropping as we went, and giving the nearest small boy fifty cents to take our copy down to the managing editor. Some of our enterprising clients, who are not habitual commuters and who live in a state of single cussedness, might try it some time.

The only thing we missed at McSorley's, we might add, was the old-time plate of onions. But then we were not there at lunch time, and the pungent fruit may have been hidden away in the famous tall ice box. Hutchins Hapgood once said, in an article about McSorley's in *Harper's Weekly:* "The wives of the men who frequent McSorley's always know where their husbands have been. There is no mistaking a McSorley onion." He was right. The McSorley onion—"rose among roots"—was *sui generis*. It had a reach and authenticity all its own.

We have said a good deal, now and then, about some of the taverns and chophouses we enjoy; but the one that tingles most strongly in our bosom is one that doesn't exist. That is the chophouse that might be put in the cellar of that glorious old round-towered building at 59 Ann Street.

As you go along Ann Street, you will come, between

numbers 57 and 61, to an old passage-way running
down to a curious courtyard, which is tenanted mostly
by carpenters and iron-workers, and by a crowded store
which seems to be a second-hand ship-chandlery, for old
sea-boots, life preservers, fenders, ship's lanterns, and
flags hang on the wall over the high stairway. In the
cellars are smithies where you will see the bright glare
of a forge and men with faces gleaming in tawny light
pulling shining irons out of the fire. The whole place is
too fascinating to be easily described. That round-
tower house is just our idea of the right place for a quiet
tavern or club, where one would go in at lunch time,
walk over a sawdusted floor to a table bleached by many
litres of slopovers, light a yard of clay, and call for
a platter of beefsteak pie. The downtown region is
greatly in need of the kind of place we have in mind, and
if any one cares to start a chophouse in that heavenly
courtyard, the Three Hours for Lunch Club pledges itself to attend regularly.

A PORTRAIT

"MY IDEA of life," said my friend S——, "would be to have a nice lawn running down to the water, several deck-chairs, plenty of tobacco, and three or four of us to sit there all day long and listen to B—— talk."

I suppose that B——,— I wish I could name him, but it would be an indecency to do so, for part of his charm is his complete unconsciousness of the affection, and even adoration, of the little group of younger men who call themselves his "fans"—I suppose that B——'s talk is as nearly Johnsonian in virtue and pungency as any spoken wisdom now hearable in this country. To know him is, in the absolute truth of that enduring phrase, a liberal education. To his simplicity, his valorous militancy for truth, he joins the mind of a great scholar, the placable spirit of an eager child.

I said "Johnsonian"—yet even in the great Doctor as we have him recorded there were a certain truculence and vehemence that are a little foreign to B——'s habit. Fearless champion as he is, there is always a gentleness about him. Even when his voice deepens and he is well launched on a long argument, he is never brutally dogmatic, never cruelly discourteous.

The beauty of B——'s talk, the quality that would make it a delight to listen to him all a summer afternoon, is that he gives, unconsciously, a perfect exhibition of a perfect process, a great mind in motion. His mind is too full, too crowded, too ratiocinative, for easy and frugal utterance. Sometimes, unless one is an acute listener, he is almost incoherent in his zeal to express all the phases and facets of the thought that flashes upon him. And yet, if one could (unknown to him) have a stenographer behind the arras to take it all down, so that his argument could be analyzed at leisure, it would show its anatomical knitting and structure. Do you remember how Burke's speech on Conciliation was parsed and subheaded in the preface to the school-texts? Just so, in I and II and III, A. B. and C, (a), (β), and (γ), i, ii, and iii, we could articulate the strict and bony logic that vertebrates B——'s talk. Reservations, exceptions, qualifications, parentheses, sub-clauses, and humorous paraphrases swim upon him as he goes, and he deals with each as it comes. Sometimes, one thinks, he has lost the spine of the discourse, is mazed in a ganglion of nerves and sinews. But no! give him time and back he comes to the marrow of his theme!

What a happiness this is to listen to—he (bless his heart) now and then apologizing for his copiousness, little dreaming that we are all better men for hearing him; that his great gray head and clear kindly eye ("His mild and magnificent eye": whose is that phrase?) are to us a symbol of Socratic virtue and power; that there is not one of us who, after an hour or so with him, does not depart with private resolutions of honour and fidelity to wisdom. How he irrigates his subject, whatever it is.

I'll tell you who Time gallops withal! It is when B—— sits down at a corner table of some chophouse, and (the rest of us seeing to it that the meal gets ordered, and now and then saying something about the food so that he will remember to eat) we marvel to watch the glow and business of a mind so great paired with a heart so simple.

"My idea is this," he says, "subject to an exception which I will state in a moment." Taking up his exception, he makes it so lucid, so pregnant, so comprehensive, so irresistible, that it seems to us the whole and satisfying dogma; and then, suddenly turning it inside-outward, he reveals the seams, and we remember that it was only a trifling nexus in the rational series. He returns to his main thesis, and other counterpoising arguments occur to him. He outlines them, with delicious Æsopian sagacity. "Of course this analysis is only quantitative, not qualitative," he says. "But

[71]

Plum Pudding

I will now restate my position with all the necessary reservations. and we'll see if it will hold water."

We smile, and look at each other slyly, in the sheer happiness of enjoying a perfect work of art. He must be a mere quintain, a poor lifeless block, who does not revel in such an exhibition, where those two rare qualities of mind—honesty and agility—are locked in one.

Of course—it is hardly necessary to say—we do not always agree with everything he says. But we could not disagree with *him;* for we see that his broad, shrewd, troubled spirit could take no other view, arising out of the very multitude and swarm and pressure of his thought. Those who plod diligently and narrowly along a country lane may sometimes reach the destination less fatigued than the more conscientious and passionate traveller who quarters the fields and beats the bounds, intent to leave no covert unscrutinized. But in him we see and love and revere something rare and precious, not often found in our present way of life; in matters concerning the happiness of others, a devoted spirit of unrivalled wisdom; in those pertaining to himself, a child's unblemished innocence. The perplexities of others are his daily study; his own pleasures, a constant surprise.

GOING TO PHILADELPHIA

I

EVERY intelligent New Yorker should be compelled, once in so often, to run over to Philadelphia and spend a few days quietly and observantly prowling.

Any lover of America is poor indeed unless he has savoured and meditated the delicious contrast of these two cities, separated by so few miles and yet by a whole world of philosophy and metaphysics. But he is a mere tyro of the two who has only made the voyage by the P. R. R. The correct way to go is by the Reading, which makes none of those annoying intermediate stops at Newark, Trenton, and so on, none of that long

detour through West Philadelphia, starts you off with
a ferry ride and a background of imperial campaniles
and lilac-hazed cliffs and summits in the superb morning light. And the Reading route, also, takes you
through a green Shakespearean land of beauty, oddly
different from the flat scrubby plains traversed by the
Pennsy. Consider, if you will, the hills of the idyllic
Huntington Valley as you near 'Philadelphia; or the
little white town of Hopewell, N. J., with its pointing
church spire. We have often been struck by the fact
that the foreign traveller between New York and Washington on the P. R. R. must think America the most
flat, dreary, and uninteresting countryside in the world.
Whereas if he would go from Jersey City by the joint
Reading—Central New Jersey—B. & O. route, how
different he would find it. No, we are not a Reading
stockholder.

We went over to Philly, after having been unfaithful to her for too many months. Now we have had
from time to time, most menacing letters from indig-
nant clients, protesting that we have been unfaithful
to all the tenets and duties of a Manhattan journalist
because we have with indecent candour confessed an
affection for both Brooklyn and Philadelphia. We
lay our cards on the table. We can't help it. Philadelphia was the first large city we ever knew, and how
she speaks to us! And there's a queer thing about
Philadelphia, hardly believable to the New Yorker
who has never conned her with an understanding eye.
You emerge from the Reading Terminal (or, if you
will, from Broad Street Station) with just a little

superbness of mood, just a tinge of worldly disdain, as feeling yourself fresh from the grandeur of Manhattan and showing perhaps (you fondly dream) some pride of metropolitan bearing. Very well. Within half an hour you will be apologizing for New York. In their quiet, serene, contented way those happy Philadelphians will be making you a little shamefaced of the bustling madness of our heaven-touching Babel. Of course, your secret adoration of Manhattan, the greatest wild poem ever begotten by the heart of man, is not readily transmissible. You will stammer something of what it means to climb upward from the subway on a spring morning and see that golden figure over Fulton Street spreading its shining wings above the new day. And they will smile gently, that knowing, amiable Philadelphia smile.

We were false to our credo in that we went via the P. R. R., but we were compensated by a man who was just behind us at the ticket window. He asked for a ticket to Asbury Park. "Single, or return?" asked the clerk. "I don't believe I'll ever come back," he said, but with so unconsciously droll an accent that the ticket seller screamed with mirth.

There was something very thrilling in strolling again along Chestnut Street, watching all those delightful people who are so unconscious of their characteristic qualities. New York has outgrown that stage entirely: New Yorkers are conscious of being New Yorkers, but Philadelphians are Philadelphians without knowing it; and hence their unique delightfulness to the observer.

Plum Pudding

Nothing seemed to us at all changed—except that the trolleys have raised their fare from five cents to seven. The Liberty Toggery Shop down on Chestnut Street was still "Going Out of Business," just as it was a couple of years ago. Philip Warner, the famous book salesman at Leary's Old Book Store, was out having lunch, as usual. The first book our eye fell upon was "The Experiences of an Irish R. M.," which we had hunted in vain in these parts. The only other book that caught our eye particularly was a copy of "Patrins," by Louise Guiney, which we saw a lady carrying on the campus of the University of Pennsylvania.

But perhaps New York exerts its own fascination upon Philadelphians, too. For when we returned we selfishly persuaded a friend of ours to ride with us on the train so that we might imbibe some of his ripe orotund philosophy, which we had long been deprived of. He is a merciless Celt, and all the way over he preached us a cogent sermon on our shortcomings and backslidings. Faithful are the wounds of a friend, and it was nice to know that there was still someone who cared enough for us to give us a sound cursing. Between times, while we were catching breath, he expatiated upon the fact that New York is death and damnation to the soul; but when we got to Manhattan Transfer he suddenly abandoned his intended plan of there catching the next train back to the land of Penn. A curious light began to gleam in his mild eyes; he settled his hat firmly upon his head and strode out into the Penn Station. "I think I'll go out and

look round a bit," he said. We wonder whether he has
gone back yet?

II

THE OTHER day we had a chance to go to Philadelphia in the right way—by the Reading, the P.
and R., the Peaceful and Rapid. As one of our
missions in life is to persuade New York and Philadelphia to love one another, we will tell you about
it.

Ah, the jolly old Reading! Take the 10 o'clock
ferry from Liberty Street, and as the *Plainfield* kicks
herself away from the slip with a churning of cream
and silver, study Manhattan's profile in the downpour
of morning sun. That winged figure on the Tel and Tel
Building (the loveliest thing in New York, we insist)
is like a huge and queerly erect golden butterfly
perched momently in the blue. The 10:12 train from
Jersey City we call the Max Beerbohm Special because
there are Seven Men in the smoker. No, the Reading
is never crowded. (Two more men did get on at Elizabeth.) You can make yourself comfortable, put your
coat, hat, and pipecleaners on one seat, your books,
papers, and matches on another. Here is the stout conductor whom we used to know so well by sight, with his
gold insignia. He has forgotten that we once travelled
with him regularly, and very likely he wonders why we
beam so cheerfully. We flash down the Bayonne penin-
sula, with a glimpse of the harbour, Staten Island in
the distance, a schooner lying at anchor. Then we
cross Newark Bay, pure opaline in a clear, pale blue

light.   H. G. Dwight is the only other chap who really
enjoys Newark Bay the way it deserves to be.   He
wrote a fine poem about it once.

But we had one great disappointment.   For an
hour or so we read a rubbishy novel, thinking to ourself that when the Max Beerbohm Express reached
that lovely Huntington Valley neighbourhood, we
would lay down the book and study the scenery, which
we know by heart.   When we came to the Neshaminy,
that blithe little green river, we were all ready to be
thrilled.   And then the train swung away to the left
along the cut-off to Wayne Junction and we missed
our bright Arcadia.   We had wanted to see again the
little cottage at Meadowbrook (so like the hunting
lodge in the forest in "The Prisoner of Zenda") which
a suasive real-estate man once tried to rent to us.
(Philadelphia realtors are no less ingenious than the
New York species.)   We wanted to see again the old
barn, rebuilt by an artist, at Bethayres, which he also
tried to rent to us.   We wanted to see again the queer
"desirable residence" (near the gas tanks at Marathon)
which he did rent us.   But we had to content ourself
with the scenery along the cut-off, which is pleasant
enough in its way—there is a brown-green brook along
a valley where a buggy was crawling down a lane
among willow trees in a wealth of sunlight.   And the
dandelions are all out in those parts.   Yes, it was a
lovely morning.   We found ourself pierced by the
kind of mysterious placid melancholy that we only enjoy
to the full in a Reading smoker, when, for some unknown reason, hymn tunes come humming into our

head and we are alarmed to notice ourself falling in love with humanity as a whole.

We could write a whole newspaper page about travelling to Philly on the Reading. Consider those little back gardens near Wayne Junction, how delightfully clean, neat, domestic, demure. Compare entering New York toward the Grand Central, down that narrow frowning alleyway of apartment house backs, with imprisoned children leaning from barred windows. But as you spin toward Wayne Junction you see acres and acres of trim little houses, each with a bright patch of turf. Here is a woman in a blue dress and white cap, busily belabouring a rug on the grass. The bank of the cutting by Wayne Junction is thick with a tangle of rosebushes which will presently be in blossom; we know them well. Spring Garden Street: if you know where to look you can catch a blink of Edgar Allan Poe's little house. Through a jumble of queer old brick chimneys and dormers, and here we are at the Reading Terminal, with its familiar bitter smell of coal gas.

Of course we stop to have a look at the engine, one of those splendid Reading locos with the three great driving wheels. Splendid things, the big Reading locos; when they halt they pant so cheerfully and noisily, like huge dogs, much louder than any other engines. We always expect to see an enormous red tongue running in and out over the cowcatcher. Vast thick pants, as the poet said in "Khubla Khan." We can't remember if he wore them, or breathed them, but there it is in the poem; look it up. Reading engineers, too, always give us a sense of security. They have gray hair, cropped very close. They have a benign look, rather like Walt Whitman if he were shaved. We wrote a poem about one of them once, Tom Hartzell, who used to take the 5:12 express out of Jersey City.

Philadelphia, incidentally, is the only large city where the Dime Museum business still flourishes. For the first thing we see on leaving the Terminal is that the old Bingham Hotel is now The World's Museum, given over to Ursa the Bear Girl and similar excitements. But where is the beautiful girl with slick dark hair who used to be at the Reading terminal news-stand?

How much more we could tell you about travelling on the Reading! We would like to tell you about the queer assortment of books we brought back with us. (There were twelve men in the smoker, coming home.) We could tell how we tried to buy, without being observed, a magazine which we will call *Foamy Fiction*, in order to see what the new editor (a friend of ours) is printing. Also, we always buy a volume of Gissing when we go to Philly, and this time we found "In the Year of Jubilee" in the shop of Jerry Cullen, the delightful bookseller who used to be so redheaded, but is getting over it now in the most logical way. We could tell you about the lovely old whitewashed stone farmhouses (with barns painted red on behalf of Schenk's Mandrake Pills) and about the famous curve near Roelofs, so called because the soup rolls off the table in the dining car when they take the curve at full speed;

and about Bound Brook, which has a prodigious dump of tin cans that catches the setting sunlight——

It makes us sad to think that a hundred years hence people will be travelling along that road and never know how much we loved it. They will be doing so to-morrow, too; but it seems more mournful to think about the people a hundred years hence.

When we got back to Jersey City, and stood on the front end of the ferryboat, Manhattan was piling up all her jewels into the cold green dusk. There were a few stars, just about as many as there are passengers in a Reading smoker. There was one big star directly over Brooklyn, and another that seemed to be just above Plainfield. We pondered, as the ferry slid toward its hutch at Liberty Street, that there were no stars above Manhattan. Just at that moment— five minutes after seven—the pinnacle of the Woolworth blossomed a ruby red. New York makes her own.

III

You never know when an adventure is going to begin. But on a train is a good place to lie in wait for them. So we sat down in the smoker of the 10 A. M. Eastern Standard Time P. R. R. express to Philadelphia, in a receptive mood.

At Manhattan Transfer the brakeman went through the train, crying in a loud, clear, emphatic barytone: "Next stop for this train is North Philadelphia!"

We sat comfortably, and in that mood of secretly exhilarated mental activity which is induced by riding on a fast train. We were looking over the June *Atlan-*

tic. We smiled gently to ourself at that unconscious
breath of New England hauteur expressed in the publisher's announcement, "*The edition of the Atlantic is
carefully restricted.*" Then, meditating also on the
admirable sense and skill with which the magazine is
edited, and getting deep into William Archer's magnificent article "The Great Stupidity" (which we hope all
our clients will read) we became aware of outcries of
anguish and suffering in the aisle near by.

At Manhattan Transfer a stout little man with a
fine domy forehead and a derby hat tilted rather far aft
had entered the smoker. He suddenly learned that the
train did not stop at Newark. He uttered lamentation,
and attacked the brakeman with grievous protest. "I
heard you say, "This train stops at Newark and Philadelphia," he insisted. His cigar revolved wildly in the
corner of his mouth; crystal beads burst out upon the
opulent curve of his forehead. "I've got to meet a man
in Newark and sell him a bill of goods."

The brakeman was gentle but firm. "Here's the conductor," he said. "You'll have to talk to him."

Now this is a tribute of admiration and respect to
that conductor. He came along the aisle punching tickets, holding his record slip gracefully folded round the
middle finger of his punch hand, as conductors do. Like
all experienced conductors he was alert, watchful, ready
for any kind of human guile and stupidity, but courteous the while. The man bound for Newark ran to him
and began his harangue. The frustrated merchant was
angry and felt himself a man with a grievance. His
voice rose in shrill tones, he waved his hands.

Going to Philadelphia

Then began a scene that was delightful to watch. The conductor was magnificently tactful. He ought to have been an ambassador (in fact, he reminded us of one ambassador, for his trim and slender figure, his tawny, drooping moustache, the gentle and serene tact of his bearing, were very like Mr. Henry van Dyke). He allowed the protestant to exhaust himself with reproaches, and then he began an affectionate little sermon, tender, sympathetic, but firm.

"I thought this train stopped at Newark," the fat man kept on saying.

"You mustn't think, you must *know*," said the conductor, gazing shrewdly at him above the rims of his demi-lune spectacles. "Now, why did you get on a train without making sure where it stopped? You heard the brakeman say: 'Newark and Philadelphia'? No; he said 'North Philadelphia.' Yes, I know you were in a hurry, but that wasn't our fault, was it? Now, let me tell you something: I've been working for this company for twenty-five years. . . ."

Unhappily the noise of the train prevented us from hearing the remark that followed. We were remembering a Chinese translation that we made once. It went something like this:

A SUSPICIOUS NATURE

Whenever I travel
I ask at least three train-men
If this is the right train
For where I am going,
Even then
I hardly believe them.

[83]

But as we watched the two, the conductor gently convincing the irate passenger that he would have to abide by his mistake, and the truculent fat man gradually realizing that he was hopelessly in the wrong, a new aspect subtly came over the dialogue. We saw the stout man wither and droop. We thought he was going to die. His hat slid farther and farther upward on his dewy brow. His hands fluttered. His cigar, grievously chewed, trembled in its corner of his mouth. His fine dark eyes filled with tears.

The conductor, you see, was explaining that he would have to pay the fare to North Philadelphia and then take the first train back from there to Newark.

We feared, for a few minutes, that it really would be a case for a chirurgeon, with cupping and leeching and smelling salts. Our rotund friend was in a bad way. His heart, plainly, was broken. From his right-hand trouser emerged a green roll. With delicate speed and tact the conductor hastened this tragic part of the performance. His silver punch flashed in his hand as he made change, issued a cash slip, and noted the name and address of the victim, for some possible future restitution, we surmised, or perhaps only as a generous anæsthetic.

The stout man sat down a few seats in front of us and we studied his back. We have never seen a more convincing display of chagrin. With a sombre introspective stare he gazed glassily before him. We never saw any one show less enthusiasm for the scenery. The train flashed busily along through the level green meadows, which blended exactly with the green plush of the seats, but our friend was lost in a gruesome trance. Even his cigar (long since gone out) was still, save for an occasional quiver.

The conductor came to our seat, looking, good man, faintly stern and sad, like a good parent who has had, regretfully, to chastise an erring urchin.

"Well," we said, "the next time that chap gets on a train he'll take care to find out where it stops."

The conductor smiled, but a humane, understanding smile. "I try to be fair with 'em," he said.

"I think you were a wonder," we said.

By the time we reached North Philadelphia the soothing hand of Time had exerted some of its consolation. The stout man wore a faintly sheepish smile as he rose to escape. The brakeman was in the vestibule. He, younger than the conductor, was no less kind, but we would hazard that he is not quite as resigned to mortal error and distress. He spoke genially, but there was a note of honest rebuke in his farewell.

"The next time you get on a train," he said, "watch your stop."

OUR TRICOLOUR TIE

WE WENT up to the composing room just now to consult our privy counsellor, Peter Augsberger, the make-up man, and after Peter had told us about his corn——

It is really astonishing, by the way, how many gardeners there are in a newspaper office. We once worked in a place where a horticultural magazine and a beautiful journal of rustic life were published, and the delightful people who edited those magazines were really men about town; but here in the teeming city and in the very node of urban affairs, to wit, the composing room, one hears nought but merry gossip about gardens, and the great and good men by whom we are surrounded begin their day by gazing tenderly upon jars full of white iris. And has not our friend Charley Sawyer of the dramatic department given us a lot of vegetable marrow seeds from his own garden and greatly embarrassed us by so doing, for he has put them in two packets marked "Male" and "Female," and to tell the truth we had no idea that the matter of sex extended even as far as the apparently placid and unperturbed vegetable marrow. Mr. Sawyer explained carefully to us just how the seeds ought to be planted, the males and females in properly wedded couples, we think he said; but we are not quite sure, and we are too modest to ask him to explain again; but if we should make a mistake in planting those seeds, if we were to—— Come, we are getting away from our topic. Peter had told us about his corn, in his garden, that is, out in Nutley (and that reminds us of the difficulties of reading poetry aloud. Mr. Chesterton tells somewhere a story about a poem of Browning's that he heard read aloud when he was a child, and understood the poem to say "John scorns ale."

Now Mr. Chesterton—you understand, of course, we are referring to Gilbert Keith Chesterton—being from his very earliest youth an avowed partisan of malt liquor, this heresy made an impression upon his tender cortex, and he never forgot about John, in Browning's poem, scorning ale. But many years afterward, reading Browning, he found that the words really were: "John's corns ail," meaning apparently that John was troubled by pedal callouses.) Peter, we repeat, and to avoid any further misunderstanding and press diligently toward our theme, having mentioned his garden, who should come up to us but Pete Corcoran, also of the composing room force, and a waggish friend of ours, and gazing on us in a manner calculated to make us feel ill at ease he said, "I suppose you are going to write something about that tie of yours."

Now we were wearing a scarf that we are very fond of, the kind of tie, we believe, that is spoken of as "regimental stripes"; at any rate, it is designated with broad diagonal bands of colour: claret, gold, and blue. It was obvious to us that Pete Corcoran, or, to give him his proper name, Mr. Corcoran, had said what he did merely in a humorous way, or possibly satiric, implying that we are generally so hard up for something to write about that we would even undertake so trifling a subject as haberdashery; but as we went downstairs again to our kennel, *au dixième*, as Mr. Wanamaker would call it, we thought seriously about this and decided that we would cause Pete's light-hearted suggestion to recoil violently upon his friendly brow, and that we would write a little essay about this tie and tell its story, which, to be honest, is very interesting to us. And this essay we are now endeavouring to write, even if it has to run in several instalments.

It was curious, incidentally (but not really more curious than most human affairs), that Pete (or Mr. Corcoran) whether he was merely chaffing us, or whether he was really curious about a scarf of such wanton colour scheme, should have mentioned it just when he did, for as a matter of fact that tie had been on our mind all morning. You see to-day being warm (and please remember that what we call to-day, is now, when you are reading this, yesterday) we did not wear our waistcoat, or, if you prefer, our vest; but by the time we had decided not to wear our waistcoat we had already tied our scarf in the usual way we tie that particular scarf when we wear it, viz., so as to conceal a certain spot on it which got there we know not how. We do not know what kind of a spot it is; perhaps it is a soup stain, perhaps it is due to a shrimp salad we had with Endymion at that amusing place that calls itself the Crystal Palace; we will not attempt to trace the origin of that swarthy blemish on the soft silk of our tie; but we have cunningly taught ourself to knot the thing so that the spot does not show. (Good, we have made that plain: we are getting along famously.)

Since the above was written we have been uptown and had lunch with Alf Harcourt and Will Howe and other merry gentlemen; and Will Howe, who used to be a professor of English and is now a publisher, says we ought to break up our essays into shorter paragraphs. We are fain and teachable, as someone once said in a very pretty poem; we will start a new paragraph right away.

But when our tie is tied in the manner described above, it leaves one end very much longer than the other. This is not noticeable when we wear our waistcoat; but having left off our waistcoat, we were fearful that the manner in which our tie was disposed would attract attention; and everyone would suspect just why it was tied in that way.

And we did not have time to take it off and put on another one, because we had to catch the 8:06.

Plum Pudding

So when Pete Corcoran spoke about our tie, was that what was in his mind, we wondered? Did he *infer* the existence of that spot, even though he did not see it? And did he therefore look down upon, or otherwise feel inclined to belittle our tie? If that were the case, we felt that we really owed it to ourself to tell the story of the tie, how we bought it, and why; and just why that tie is to us not merely a strip of rather gaudy neckwear, but a symbol of an enchanting experience, a memory and token of an epoch in our life, the sign and expression of a certain feeling that can never come again— and, indeed (as the sequel will show), that should not have come when it did.

It was a bright morning, last November, in Gloversville, New York, when we bought that tie. Now an explanation of just why we bought that tie, and what we were doing in Gloversville, cannot possibly be put into a paragraph, at any rate the kind of paragraph that Will Howe (who used to be a professor of English) would approve. On the whole, rather than rewrite the entire narrative, tersely, we will have to postpone the dénouement (of the story, not the tie) until to-morrow. This is an exhibition of the difficulty of telling anything exactly. There are so many subsidiary considerations that beg for explanation. Please be patient, Pete, and to-morrow we will explain that tie in detail.

II

It was a bright and transparent cold morning in Gloversville, N. Y., November, 1919, and passing out of the Kingsborough Hotel we set off to have a look at

[90]

the town. And if we must be honest, we were in passable good humour. To tell the ruth, as Gloversville began its daily tasks in that clear lusty air and in a white dazzling sunshine, we believed, simpleton that we were, that we were on the road toward making our fortune. Now, we will have to be brief in explanation of the reason why we felt so, for it is a matter not easy to discuss with the requisite delicacy. Shortly, we were on the road—"trouping," they call it in the odd and glorious world of the theatre—with a little play in which we were partially incriminated, on a try-out voyage of one-night stands. The night before, the company had played Johnstown (a few miles from Gloversville), and if we do have to say it, the good-natured citizens of that admirable town had given them an enthusiastic reception. So friendly indeed had been our houses on the road and so genially did the company manager smile upon us that any secret doubts and qualms we had entertained were now set at rest. Lo! had not the company manager himself condescended to share a two-room suite with us in the Kingsborough Hotel that night? And we, a novice in this large and exhilarating tract of life, thought to ourself that this was the ultimate honour that could be conferred upon a lowly co-author. Yes, we said to ourself, as we beamed upon the excellent town of Gloversville, admiring the Carnegie Library and the shops and the numerous motor cars and the bright shop windows and munching some very fine doughnuts we had seen in a bakery. Yes, we repeated, this is the beginning of fame and fortune. Ah! Pete Corcoran may scoff, but that was a bright and golden

morning, and we would not have missed it. We did
not know then the prompt and painful end destined for
that innocent piece when it reached the Alba Via Max-
ima. All we knew was that Saratoga and Newburgh
and Johnstown had taken us to their bosoms.

At this moment, and our thoughts running thus,
we happened to pass by the window of a very alluring
haberdasher's shop. In that window we saw displayed
a number of very brilliant neckties, all rich and glowing
with bright diagonal stripes. The early sunlight fell
upon them and they were brave to behold. And we
said to ourself that it would be a proper thing for one
who was connected with the triumphal onward march
of a play that was knocking them cold on the one-night
circuit to flourish a little and show some sign of worldly
vanity. (We were still young, that November, and our
mind was still subject to some harmless frailties.)
We entered the shop and bought that tie, the very same
one that struck Pete Corcoran with a palsy when he saw
it the other day. We put it in our pocket and walked
back to the hotel.

Now comes a portion of the narrative that exhibits to
the full the deceits and stratagems of the human being.
This tie, which we liked so much, thinking it the kind
of thing that would add a certain dash and zip to our
bearing, was eminently a metropolitan-looking kind of
scarf. No one would think to look at it that it had
been bought in Gloversville. And we said to ourself
that if we went quietly back to the hotel and slipped un-
obtrusively into the washroom and put on that tie, no
one would know that we had just bought it in Glovers-

ville, but would think it was a part of our elaborate
wardrobe that we had brought from New York.   Very
well.   (We would not reveal these shameful subterfuges
to any one but Pete Corcoran.)   No sooner said than
done; and behold us taking the trolley from Gloversville to Fonda, with the rest of the company, wearing
that tie that flared and burned in the keen wintry light
like a great banner, like an oriflamme of youthful defiance.

And what a day that was!   We shall never forget it;
we will never forget it!   Was that the Mohawk Valley
that glittered in the morning?   (A sunshine so bright
that sitting on the sunward side of the smoker and
lighting our pipe, the small flame of our match paled
shamefully into a tiny and scarce visible ghost.)   Our
tie strengthened and sustained us in our zest for a world
so coloured and contoured.   We even thought that it
was a bit of a pity that our waistcoat was cut with so
shallow and conservative a V that the casual passerby
would see but little of that triumphant silk beacon.
The fellow members of our company were too polite
to remark upon it, but we saw that they had noticed it
and took it as a joyful omen.

We had two and a half hours in Albany that day
and we remember that we had set our heart on buying a
certain book.   Half an hour we allotted to lunch and
the other two hours was spent in visiting the bookshops
of Albany, which are many and good.   We wonder if
any Albany booksellers chance to recall a sudden flash
of colour that came, moved along the shelves, and was
gone?   We remember half a dozen book stores that we

visited; we remember them just as well as if it were
yesterday, and we remember the great gusto and
bright cheer of the crowds of shoppers, already doing
their Christmas pioneering. We remember also that
three of the books we bought (to give away) were Mc-
Fee's "Aliens" and Frank Adams's "Tobogganing on
Parnassus," yes, and Stevenson's "Lay Morals." Oh, a
great day! And we remember the ride from Albany to
Kingston, with the darkening profile of the Catskills on
the western side of the train, the tawny colours of the
fields (like a lion's hide), the blue shadows of the glens,
the sparkling Hudson in quick blinks of brightness, the
lilac line of the hills when we reached Kingston in the
dusk. We remember the old and dilapidated theatre
at Kingston, the big shabby dressing rooms of the men,
with the scribbled autographs of former mummers on
the walls. And that night we said good-bye to our
little play, whose very imperfections we had grown to
love by this time, and took the 3:45 A. M. milk train
to New York. We slept on two seats in the smoker,
and got to Weehawken in the brumous chill of a winter
dawn—still wearing our tie. Now can Pete Corcoran
wonder why we are fond of it, and why, ever and anon,
we get it out and wear it in remembrance?

THE CLUB OF ABANDONED HUSBANDS

AJAX: Hullo, Socrates, what are you doing patrolling the streets at this late hour? Surely it would be more seemly to be at home?

SOCRATES: You speak sooth, Ajax, but I have no home to repair to.

AJAX: What do you mean by that?

SOCRATES: In the sense of a place of habitation, a dormitory, of course I still have a home; but it is merely an abandoned shell, a dark and silent place devoid of allure. I have sent my family to the seashore, good Ajax, and the lonely apartment, with all the blinds pulled down and nothing in the icebox, is a dismal haunt. That is why I wander upon the highway.

Plum Pudding

AJAX: I, too, have known that condition, Socrates. Two years ago Cassandra took the children to the mountains for July and August; and upon my word I had a doleful time of it. What do you say, shall we have recourse to a beaker of ginger ale and discuss this matter? It is still only the shank of the evening.

SOCRATES: It is well thought of.

AJAX: As I was saying, the quaint part of it was that before my wife left I had secretly thought that a period of bachelorhood would be an interesting change. I rather liked the idea of strolling about in the evenings, observing the pageant of human nature in my quiet way, dropping in at the club or the library, and mingling with my fellow men in a fashion that the husband and father does not often have opportunity to do.

SOCRATES: And when Cassandra went away you found yourself desolate?

AJAX: Even so. Of course matters were rather different in those days, before the archons had taken away certain stimulants, but the principle is still the same. You know, the inconsistency of man is rather entertaining. I had often complained about having to help put the children to bed when I got home from the office. I grudged the time it took to get them all safely bestowed. And then, when the children were away, I found myself spending infinitely more time and trouble in getting some of my bachelor friends to bed.

SOCRATES: As that merry cartoonist Briggs observes in some of his frescoes, Oh Man!

AJAX: I wonder if your experience is the same as mine was? I found that about six o'clock in the eve-

The Club of Abandoned Husbands

ning, the hour when I would normally have been hasten-ing home to wife and babes, was the most poignant time. I was horribly homesick. If I did go back to my forlorn apartment, the mere sight of little Priam's crib was enough to reduce me to tears. I seriously thought of writing a poem about it.

SOCRATES: What is needed is a Club of Abandoned Husbands, for the consolation of those whose families are out of town.

AJAX: I have never found a club of much assistance at such a time. It is always full of rather elderly men who talk a great deal and in a manner both doleful and ill-informed.

SOCRATES: But this would be a club of quite a different sort. It would be devised to offer a truly domestic atmosphere to those who have sent their wives and juveniles to the country for the benefit of the fresh air, and have to stay in the city themselves to earn what is vulgarly known as kale.

AJAX: How would you work out the plan?

SOCRATES: It would not be difficult. In the first place, there would be a large nursery, with a number of rented children of various ages. Each member of the club, hastening thither from his office at the conclusion of the day's work, would be privileged to pick out some child as nearly as possible similar in age and sex to his own absent offspring. He would then deal with this child according to the necessities of its condition. If it were an extremely young infant, a bottle properly prepared would be ready in the club kitchen, and he could administer it. The club bathroom would be filled with hilarious members on their knees beside small tubs, bathing such urchins as needed it. Others would be playing games on the floor, or tucking the children in bed. It ought to be quite feasible to hire a number of children for this purpose. During the day they would be cared for by a competent matron. Baby carriages would be provided, and if any of the club members were compelled to remain in town over the week-end they could take the children for an airing in the park.

AJAX: This is a brave idea, Socrates. And then, when all the children were bedded for the night, how would the domestic atmosphere be simulated?

SOCRATES: Nothing simpler. After dinner such husbands as are accustomed to washing the dishes would be allowed to do so in the club kitchen. During the day it would be the function of the matron to think up a number of odd jobs to be performed in the course of the evening. Pictures would be hung, clocks wound, a number of tin cans would be waiting to be opened with refractory can openers, and there would always be several window blinds that had gone wrong. A really resourceful matron could devise any number of ways of making the club seem just like home. One night she would discern a smell of gas, the next there might be a hole in the fly-screens, or a little carpentering to do, or a caster broken under the piano. Husbands with a turn for plumbing would find the club basement a perpetual place of solace, with a fresh leak or a rumbling pipe every few days.

AJAX: Admirable! And if the matron really wanted to make the members feel at home she would take a

The Club of Abandoned Husbands

turn through the building every now and then, to issue a gentle rebuke for cigar ashes dropped on the rugs or feet elevated on chairs.

SOCRATES: The really crowning touch, I think, would lie in the ice-box raids. A large ice-box would be kept well stocked with remainders of apple pie, macaroni, stewed prunes, and chocolate pudding. Any husband, making a cautious inroad upon these about midnight, would surely have the authentic emotion of being in his own home.

AJAX: An occasional request to empty the ice-box pan would also be an artful echo of domesticity.

SOCRATES: Of course the success of the scheme would depend greatly on finding the right person for matron. If she were to strew a few hairpins about and perhaps misplace a latch key now and then——

AJAX: Socrates, you have hit upon a great idea. But you ought to extend the membership of the club to include young men not yet married. Think what an admirable training school for husbands it would make!

SOCRATES: My dear fellow, let us not discuss it any further. It makes me too homesick. I am going back to my lonely apartment to write a letter to dear Xanthippe.

WEST BROADWAY

DID you ever hear of Finn Square? No? Very
well, then, we shall have to inflict upon you some
paragraphs from our unpublished work: "A Scenic
Guidebook to the Sixth Avenue L." The itinerary is a
frugal one: you do not have to take the L, but walk
along under it.

Streets where an L runs have a fascination of their
own. They have a shadowy gloom, speckled and
striped with the sunlight that slips through the trestles.
West Broadway, which along most of its length is
straddled by the L, is a channel of odd humours. Its
real name, you know, is South Fifth Avenue; but the
Avenue got so snobbish it insisted on its humbler
brother changing its name. Let us take it from Spring
Street southward.

West Broadway

Ribbons, purple, red, and green, were the first thing to catch our eye. Not the ribbons of the milliner, however, but the carbon tapes of the typewriter, big cans of them being loaded on a junk wagon. "Purple Ribbons" we have often thought, would be a neat title for a volume of verses written on a typewriter. What happens to the used ribbons of modern poets? Mr. Hilaire Belloc, or Mr. Chesterton, for instance. Give me but what these ribbons type and all the rest is merely tripe, as Edmund Waller might have said. Near the ribbons we saw a paper-box factory, where a number of high-spirited young women were busy at their machines. A broad strip of thick green paint was laid across the lower half of the windows so that these immured damsels might not waste their employers' time in watching goings on along the pavement.

Broome and Watts streets diverge from West Broadway in a V. At the corner of Watts is one of West Broadway's many saloons, which by courageous readjustments still manage to play their useful part. What used to be called the "Business Men's Lunch" now has a tendency to name itself "Luncheonette" or "Milk Bar." But the old decorations remain. In this one you will see the electric fixtures wrapped in heavy lead foil, the kind of sheeting that is used in packages of tea. At the corner of Grand Street is the Sapphire Café, and what could be a more appealing name than that? "Delicious Chocolate with Whipped Cream," says a sign outside the Sapphire. And some way farther down (at the corner of White Street) is a jolly old tavern which looked so antique and inviting that we went inside. Little tables piled high with hunks of bread betokened the approaching lunch hour. A shimmering black cat winked a drowsy topaz eye from her lounge in the corner. We asked for cider. There was none, but our gaze fell upon a bottle marked "Irish Moss." We asked for some, and the barkeep pushed the bottle forward with a tiny glass. Irish Moss, it seems, is the kind of drink which the customer pours out for himself, so we decanted a generous slug. It proved to be a kind of essence of horehound, of notable tartness and pungency, very like a powerful cough syrup. We wrote it off on our ledger as experience. Beside us stood a sturdy citizen with a freight hook round his neck, deducing a foaming crock of the legitimate percentage.

The chief landmark of that stretch of West Broadway is the tall spire of St. Alphonsus' Church, near Canal Street. Up the steps and through plain brown doors we went into the church, which was cool, quiet, and empty, save for a busy charwoman with humorous Irish face. Under the altar canopy wavered a small candle spark, and high overhead, in the dimness, were orange and scarlet gleams from a stained window. A crystal chandelier hanging in the aisle caught pale yellow tinctures of light. No Catholic church, wherever you find it, is long empty; a man and a girl entered just as we went out. At each side of the front steps the words *Copiosa apud eum redemtio* are carved in the stone. The mason must have forgotten the *p* in the last word. A silver plate on the brick house next door says *Redemptorist Fathers*.

West Broadway

York Street, running off to the west, gives a glimpse of the old Hudson River Railroad freight depot. St. John's Lane, running across York Street, skirts the ruins of old St. John's Church, demolished when the Seventh Avenue subway was built. On the old brown house at the corner some urchin has chalked the word CRAZY. Perhaps this is an indictment of adult civilization as a whole. If one strolls thoughtfully about some of these streets—say Thompson Street—on a hot day, and sees the children struggling to grow up, he feels like going back to that word CRAZY and italicizing it. The tiny triangle of park at Beach Street is carefully locked up, you will notice—the only plot of grass in that neighbourhood—so that bare feet cannot get at it. Superb irony of circumstance: on the near corner stands the Castoria factory, Castoria being (if we remember the ads) what Mr. Fletcher gave baby when she was sick.

Where Varick Street runs in there is a wide triangular spread, and this, gentle friends, is Finn Park, named for a New York boy who was killed in France. The name reminded us also of Elfin Finn, the somewhat complacent stage child who poses for chic costumes in *Vogue*. We were wondering which was a more hazardous bringing up for a small girl, living on Thompson Street or posing for a fashion magazine. From Finn Square there is a stirring view of the Woolworth Tower. Also of Claflin's packing cases on their way off to Selma, Ala., and Kalamazoo, Mich., and to Nathan Povich, Bath, Me. That conjunction of Finn and Bath, Me., suggested to us that the empty space there would be a good place to put in a municipal swimming pool for the urchins of the district.

Drawn from the wood, which legend still stands on the pub at the corner of Duane Street, sounds a bit ominous these wood alcohol days. John Barleycorn may be down, but he's never out, as someone has remarked. For near Murray Street you will find one of those malt-and-hops places which are getting numerous. They contain all the necessary equipment for—well, as the signs suggest, for making malt bread and coffee cake—bottle-capping apparatus and rubber tubing and densimeters, and all such things used in breadmaking. As the signs say: "Malt syrup for making malt bread, coffee, cake, and medicinal purposes."

To conclude the scenic pleasures of the Sixth Avenue L route, we walk through the cool, dark, low-roofed tunnel of Church Street in those interesting blocks just north of Vesey. We hark to the merry crowing of the roosters in the Barclay Street poultry stores; and we look past the tall gray pillars of St. Peter's Church at the flicker of scarlet and gold lights near the altar. The black-robed nuns one often sees along Church Street, with their pale, austere, hooded faces, bring a curious touch of medievalism into the roaring tide that flows under the Hudson Terminal Building. They always walk in twos, which seems to indicate an even greater apprehension of the World. And we always notice, as we go by the pipe shop at the corner of Barclay Street, that this worthy merchant has painted some inducements on one side of his shop; which reminds us of the same device used by the famous tobacconist Bacon, in Cambridge, England. Why, we wonder, doesn't our friend fill the remaining blank panel on his side wall by painting there some stanzas from Calverley's "Ode to Tobacco?" We will gladly give him the text to copy if he wants it.

THE RUDENESS OF POETS

THE poet who has not learned how to be rude has not learned his first duty to himself. By "poet" I mean, of course, any imaginative creator—novelist, mathematician, editor, or a man like Herbert Hoover. And by "rude" I mean the strict and definite limitation which, sooner or later, he must impose upon his sociable instincts. He must refuse to fritter away priceless time and energy in the random genialities of the world. Friendly, well-meaning, and fumbling hands will stretch out to bind the poet's heart in the maddening pack-thread of Lilliput. It will always be so. Life, for most, is so empty of consecrated purpose, so full of palaver, that they cannot understand the trouble of one who carries a flame in his heart, and whose salvation depends on his strength

The Rudeness of Poets

to nourish that flame unsuffocated by crowding and scrutiny.

The poet lives in an alien world. That is not his pride; it is his humility. It is often his joy, but often also his misery: he must dree his weird. His necessary solitude of spirit is not luxury, nor the gesture of a churl: it is his sacrifice, it is the condition on which he lives. He must be content to seem boorish to the general in order to be tender to his duty. He has invisible guests at the table of his heart: those places are reserved against all comers. He must be their host first of all, or he is damned. He serves the world by cutting it when they meet inopportunely. There are times (as Keats said and Christ implied) when the wind and the stars are his wife and children.

There will be a thousand pressures to bare his bosom to the lunacy of public dinners, lecture platforms, and what not pleasant folderol. He must be privileged apparent ruffian discourtesy. He has his own heart-burn to consider. One thinks of Rudyard Kipling in this connection. Mr. Kipling stands above all other men of letters to-day in the brave clearness with which he has made it plain that he consorts first of all with his own imagination.

As the poet sees the world, and studies, the more he realizes that men are sharply cut in two classes: those who understand, those who do not. With the latter he speaks a foreign language and with effort, trying shamefacedly to conceal his strangeness. With these, perhaps, every moment spent is for ever lost. With the others he can never commune enough, seeking clumsily to share and impart those moments of rare intuition when truth came near. There is rarely any doubt as to this human division: the heart knows its kin.

The world, as he sees it around him, is almost unconscious of its unspeakable loveliness and mystery; and it is largely regimented and organized for absurdity. The greater part of the movement he sees is (by his standard) not merely stupid (which is pardonable and appealing), but meaningless altogether. He views it between anger and tenderness. Where there might have been the exquisite and delicious simplicity of a Japanese print, he sees the flicker and cruel garishness of a speeding film. And so, for refreshment, he crosses through the invisible doorway into his own dear land of lucidity. He cons over that passport of his unsociability, words of J. B. Yeats which should be unforgotten in every poet's mind:

Poetry is the voice of the solitary man. The poet is always a solitary; and yet he speaks to others—he would win their attention. Thus it follows that every poem is a social act done by a solitary man. And being an alien from the strange land of the solitary, he cannot be expected to admonish or to sermonize, or uplift, as it is called; and so take part in the cabals and intrigues in other lands of which he knows nothing, being himself a stranger from a strange land, the land of the solitary. People listen to him as they would to any other traveller come from distant countries, and all he asks for is courtesy even as he himself is courteous.

Inferior poets are those who forget their dignity— and, indeed, their only chance of being permitted to

The Rudeness of Poets

live—and to make friends try to enter into the lives of the people whom they would propitiate, and so become teachers and moralists and preachers. And soon for penalty of their rashness and folly they forget their own land of the solitary, and its speech perishes from their lips. The traveller's tales are of all the most precious, because he comes from a land—the poet's solitude—which no other feet have trodden and which no other feet will tread.

So, briefly and awkwardly, he justifies himself, being given (as Mrs. Quickly apologized) to "allicholy and musing." Oh, it is not easy! As Gilbert Chesterton said, in a noble poem:

> The way is all so very plain
> That we may lose the way.

1100 WORDS

THE managing editor, the city editor, the production manager, the foreman of the composing room, and the leading editorial writer having all said to us with a great deal of sternness, "Your copy for Saturday has got to be upstairs by such and such a time, because we are going to make up the page at so and so A. M.," we got rather nervous.

If we may say so, we did not like the way they said it. They spoke—and we are thinking particularly of the production manager—with a kind of paternal severity that was deeply distressing to our spirit. They are all, in off hours, men of delightfully easy disposition. They are men with whom it would be a pleasure and a privilege to be cast away on a desert island or in a

crowded subway train. It is only just to say that they
are men whom we admire greatly. When we meet
them in the elevator, or see them at Frank's having
lunch, how full of jolly intercourse they are. But
in the conduct of their passionate and perilous business, that is, of getting the paper out on time, a holy
anguish shines upon their brows. The stern daughter
of the voice of God has whispered to them, and
they pass on the whisper to us through a mega-
phone.

That means to say that within the hour we have
got to show up something in the neighbourhood of 1100
words to these magistrates and overseers. With these
keys—typewriter keys, of course—we have got to un-
lock our heart. Milton, thou shouldst be living at this
hour. Speaking of Milton, the damp that fell round
his path (in Wordsworth's sonnet) was nothing to the
damp that fell round our alert vestiges as we hastened
to the Salamis station in that drench this morning.
(We ask you to observe our self-restraint. We might
have said "drenching downpour of silver Long Island
rain," or something of that sort, and thus got several
words nearer our necessary total of 1100. But we
scorn, even when writing against time, to take petty
advantages. Let us be brief, crisp, packed with
thought. Let it stand as drench, while you admire
our proud conscience.)

Eleven hundred words—what a lot could be said
in 1100 words! We stood at the front door of the
baggage car (there is an odd irony in this: the leading
editorial writer, one of the most implacable of our

taskmasters, is spending the summer at Sea Cliff, and he gets the last empty seat left in the smoker. So we, getting on at Salamis, have to stand in the baggage car) watching the engine rock and roar along the rails, while the rain sheeted the level green fields. It is very agreeable to ride on a train in the rain. We have never known just why, but it conduces to thought. The clear trickles of water are drawn slantwise across the window panes, and one watches, absently, the curious behaviour of the drops. They hang bulging and pendulous, in one spot for some seconds. Then, as they swell, suddenly they break loose and zigzag swiftly down the pane, following the slippery pathway that previous drops have made. It is like a little puzzle game where you manœuvre a weighted capsule among pegs toward a narrow opening. "Pigs in clover," they sometimes call it, but who knows why? The conduct of raindrops on a smoking-car window is capricious and odd, but we must pass on. That topic alone would serve for several hundred words, but we will not be opportunist.

We stood at the front door of the baggage car, and in a pleasant haze of the faculties we thought of a number of things. We thought of some books we had seen up on East Fifty-ninth Street, in that admirable row of old bookshops, particularly Mowry Saben's volume of essays, "The Spirit of Life," which we are going back to buy one of these days; so please let it alone. We then got out a small note-book in which we keep memoranda of books we intend to read and pored over it zealously. Just for fun, we will tell you three of the titles we have noted there:

"The Voyage of the Hoppergrass," by E. L. Pearson.
"People and Problems," by Fabian Franklin.
"Broken Stowage," by David W. Bone.

But most of all we thought, in a vague sentimental way, about that pleasant Long Island country through which the engine was haling and hallooing all those carloads of audacious commuters.

Only the other day we heard a wise man say that he did not care for Long Island, because one has to travel through a number of half-built suburbs before getting into real country. We felt, when he said it, that it would be impossible for us to tell him how much some of those growing suburbs mean to us, for we have lived in them. There is not one of those little frame dwellings that doesn't give us a thrill as we buzz past them. If you voyage from Brooklyn, as we do, you will have noticed two stations (near Jamaica) called Clarenceville and Morris Park. Now we have never got off at those stations, though we intend to some day. But in those rows of small houses and in sudden glimpses of modest tree-lined streets and corner drug stores we can see something that we are not subtle enough to express. We see it again in the scrap of green park by the station at Queens, and in the brave little public library near the same station—which we cannot see from the train, though we often try to; but we know it is there, and probably the same kindly lady librarian and the children borrowing books. We see it again—

or we did the other day—in a field at Mineola where a number of small boys were flying kites in the warm, clean, softly perfumed air of a July afternoon. We see it in the vivid rows of colour in the florist's meadow at Floral Park. We don't know just what it is, but over all that broad tract of hardworking suburbs there is a secret spirit of practical and persevering decency that we somehow associate with the soul of America.

We see it with the eye of a lover, and we know that it is good.

Having got as far as this, we took the trouble to count all the words up to this point. The total is exactly 1100.

SOME INNS

THE other evening we went with Titania to a ramshackle country hotel which calls itself *The Mansion House*, looking forward to a fine robust meal. It was a transparent, sunny, cool evening, and when we saw on the bill of fare *half broiled chicken*, we innocently supposed that the word *half* was an adjective modifying the compound noun, *broiled-chicken*. Instead, to our sorrow and disappointment, it proved to be an adverb modifying *broiled* (we hope we parse the matter correctly). At any rate, the wretched fowl was blue and pallid, a little smoked on the exterior, raw and sinewy within, and an affront to the whole profession of innkeeping. Whereupon, in the days that followed, looking back at our fine mood of expectancy as we entered that hostelry, and its pitiable collapse when the miserable travesty of victuals was laid before us, we fell to thinking about some of the inns we had known

[115]

of old time where we had feasted not without good heart.

To speak merely by sudden memory, for instance, there was the fine old hotel in Burlington, Vermont— is it called the *Van Ness House?*—where we remember a line of cane-bottomed chairs on a long shady veranda, where one could look out and see the town simmering in that waft of hot and dazzling sunshine that pours across Lake Champlain in the late afternoon: and *The Black Lion*, Lavenham, Suffolk; where (unless we confuse it with a pub in Bury St. Edmunds where we had lunch), there was, in the hallway, a very fine old engraving called "Pirates Decoying a Merchantman," in which one pirate, dressed in woman's clothes, stood up above the bulwarks waving for assistance, while the cutlassed ruffians crouched below ready to do their bloody work when the other ship came near enough. Nor have we forgotten *The Saracen's Head*, at Ware, whence we went exploring down the little river Lea on Izaak Walton's trail; nor *The Swan* at Bibury in Gloucestershire, hard by that clear green water the Colne; nor another *Swan* at Tetsworth in Oxfordshire, which one reaches after bicycling over the beechy slope of the Chilterns, and where, in the narrow taproom, occurred the fabled encounter between a Texas Rhodes Scholar logged with port wine and seven Oxfordshire yokels who made merry over his power of carrying the red blood of the grape.

Our friend C. F. B., while we were meditating these golden matters, wrote to us that he is going on a walking or bicycling trip in England next summer, and asks for suggestions. We advise him to get a copy of Muirhead's "England" (the best general guidebook we have seen) and look up his favourite authors in the index. That will refer him to the places associated with them, and he can have rare sport in hunting them out. There is no way of pilgrimage so pleasant as to follow the spoor of a well-loved writer. Referring to our black note-book, in which we keep memoranda of a modest pilgrimage we once made to places mentioned by two of our heroes, viz., Boswell and R. L. S., we think that if we were in C. F. B.'s shoes, one of the regions we would be most anxious to revisit would be Dove Dale, in Derbyshire. This exquisite little valley is reached from Ashbourne, where we commend the *Green Man Inn* (visited more than once by Doctor Johnson and Boswell). This neighbourhood also has memories of George Eliot, and of Izaak Walton, who used to go fishing in the little river Dove; his fishing house is still there. Unfortunately, when we were in those parts we did not have sense enough to see the Manyfold, a curious stream (a tributary of the Dove) which by its habit of running underground caused Johnson and Boswell to argue about miracles.

Muirhead's book will give C. F. B. sound counsel about the inns of that district, which are many and good. The whole region of the Derbyshire Peak is rarely visited by the foreign tourist. Of it, Doctor Johnson, with his sturdy prejudice, said: "He who has seen Dove Dale has no need to visit the Highlands." The metropolis of this moorland is Buxton: unhappily we did not make a note of the inn we visited in that town; but we have a clear recollection of claret, candle-light, and reading "Weir of Hermiston" in bed; also a bathroom with hot water, not too common in the cheap hostelries we frequented.

We can only wish for the good C. F. B. as happy an evening as we spent (with our eccentric friend Mifflin McGill) bicycling from the *Newhaven Inn* in a July twilight. The *Newhaven Inn*, which is only a vile kind of meagre roadhouse at a lonely fork in the way (where one arm of the signpost carries the romantic legend "To Haddon Hall"), lies between Ashbourne and Buxton. But it is marked on all the maps, so perhaps it has an honourable history. The sun was dying in red embers over the Derbyshire hills as we pedalled along. Life, liquor, and literature lay all before us; certes, we had no thought of ever writing a daily column! And finally, after our small lanterns were lit and cast their little fans of brightness along the flowing road, we ascended a rise and saw Buxton in the valley below, twinkling with lights—

> "*And when even dies, the million-tinted,*
> *And the night has come, and planets glinted*
> *Lo, the valley hollow*
> *Lamp-bestarred!*"

Nor were all these ancient inns (to which our heart wistfully returns) on British soil. There was the *Hotel de la Tour*, in Montjoie, a quaint small town somewhere in that hilly region of the Ardennes along the border between Luxemburg and Belgium. Our mem-

ory is rather vague as to Montjoie, for we got there late
one evening, after more than seventy up-and-down
miles on a bicycle, hypnotic with weariness and the
smell of pine trees and a great warm wind that had
buffeted us all day. But we have a dim, comfortable
remembrance of a large clean bedroom, unlighted, in
which we duskily groped and found no less than three
huge beds among which we had to choose; and we can
see also a dining room brilliantly papered in scarlet, with
good old prints on the walls and great wooden beams
overhead. Two bottles of ice-cold beer linger in our
thought: and there was some excellent work done on a
large pancake, one of those durable fleshy German
Pfannkuchen. For the odd part of it was (unless our
memory is wholly amiss) Montjoie was then (1912)
supposed to be part of Germany, and they pronounced
it Mon-yowey. But the Reich must have felt that this
was not permanent, for they had not Germanized either
the name of the town or of the hostelry.

And let us add, in this affectionate summary, *The
Lion—(Hotel zum Löwen)*—at Sigmaringen, that delicious little haunt on the upper Danube, where the
castle sits on a stony jut overlooking the river. Alger-
non Blackwood, in one of his superb tales of fantasy
(in the volume called "The Listener") has told a fascinating gruesome story of the Danube, describing a
sedgy, sandy, desolate region below the Hungarian
border where malevolent inhuman forces were apparent
and resented mortal intrusion. But we cannot testify to anything sinister in the bright water of the Danube in the flow of its lovely youth, above Sigmaringen.

And if there were any evil influences, surely at Sigmaringen (the ancient home and origin of the Hohenzollerns, we believe) they would have shown themselves. In those exhilarating miles of valley, bicycled in company with a blithe vagabond who is now a professor at Cornell, we learned why the waltz was called "The Blue Danube." So heavenly a tint of transparent blue-green we have never seen elsewhere, the hurrying current sliding under steep crags of gray and yellow stone, whitened upon sudden shallows into long terraces of broken water. There was a wayside chapel with painted frescoes and Latin inscriptions (why didn't we make a note of them, we wonder?) and before it a cold gush sluicing from a lion's mouth into a stone basin. A blue crockery mug stood on the rim, and the bowl was spotted with floating petals from pink and white rose-bushes. We can still see our companion, tilting a thirsty bearded face as he drank, outlined on such a backdrop of pure romantic beauty as only enriches irresponsible youth in its commerce with the world. The river bends sharply to the left under a prodigious cliff, where is some ancient castle or religious house. There he stands, excellent fellow, forever (in our memory) holding that blue mug against a Maxfield Parrish scene.

Just around that bend, if you are discreet, a bathe can be accomplished, and you will reach the *Lion* by supper time, vowing the Danube the loveliest of all streams.

Of the *Lion* itself, now that we compress the gland of memory more closely, we have little to report save a general sensation of cheerful comfort. That in itself is

Some Inns

favourable: the bad inns are always accurately tabled in mind. But stay—here is a picture that unexpectedly presents itself. On that evening (it was July 15, 1912) there was a glorious little girl, about ten years old, taking supper at the *Lion* with her parents. Through the yellow shine of the lamps she suddenly reappears to us, across the dining room—rather a more luxurious dining room than the two wayfarers were accustomed to visit. We can see her straight white frock, her plump brown legs in socks (not reaching the floor as she sat), her tawny golden hair with a red ribbon. The two dusty vagabonds watched her, and her important-looking adults, from afar. We have only the vaguest impression of her father: he was erect and handsome and not untouched with pride. (Heavens, were they some minor offshoot of the Hohenzollern tribe?) We can see the head waiter smirking near their table. Across nine years and thousands of miles they still radiate to us a faint sense of prosperity and breeding; and the child was like a princess in a fairy-tale. Ah, if only it had all been a fairy-tale. Could we but turn back the clock to that summer evening when the dim pine-alleys smelled so resinous on the Muehlberg, turn back the flow of that quick blue river, turn back history itself and rewrite it in chapters fit for the clear eyes of that child we saw.

Well, we are growing grievous: it is time to go out and have some cider. There are many other admirable inns we might soliloquize—The *Seven Stars* in Rotterdam (Molensteeg 19, "nabij het Postkantoor"); *Gibson's Hotel*, Rutland Square, Edinburgh ("Well adapted

[121]

for Marriages," says its card); the *Hotel Davenport*, Stamford, Connecticut, where so many palpitating playwrights have sat nervously waiting for the opening performance; the *Tannhäuser Hotel* in Heidelberg, notable for the affability of the chambermaids. Perhaps you will permit us to close by quoting a description of an old Irish tavern, from that queer book "The Life of John Buncle, Esq." (1756). This inn bore the curious name *The Conniving House:*

The *Conniving-House* (as the gentlemen of Trinity called it in my time, and long after) was a little public house, kept by *Jack Macklean*, about a quarter of a mile beyond Rings-end, on the top of the beach, within a few yards of the sea. Here we used to have the finest fish at all times; and in the season, green peas, and all the most excellent vegetables. The ale here was always extraordinary, and everything the best; which, with its delightful situation, rendered it a delightful place of a summer's evening. Many a delightful evening have I passed in this pretty thatched house with the famous *Larrey Grogan*, who played on the bagpipes extreme well; dear *Jack Lattin*, matchless on the fiddle, and the most agreeable of companions; that ever charming young fellow, *Jack Wall* . . . and many other delightful fellows; who went in the days of their youth to the shades of eternity. When I think of them and their evening songs—*We will go to Johnny Macklean's*—*to try if his ale be good or no*, etc., and that years and infirmities begin to oppress me— What is life!

There is a fine, easy, mellow manner of writing, worthy the subject. And we—we conclude with honest regret. Even to write down the names of all the inns where we have been happy would be the pleas- antest possible way of spending an afternoon. But we advise you to be cautious in adopting our favourites as stopping places. Some of them are very humble.

THE CLUB IN HOBOKEN

THE advertisement ran as follows:

Schooner *Hauppauge*
For Sale
By U. S. Marshal,
April 26, 1 p. m.,
Pier G, Erie R. R.,
Weehawken, N. J.
Built at Wilmington, N. C., 1918; net
tonnage 1,295; length 228; equipped with
sails, tackle, etc.

This had taken the eye of the Three Hours for Lunch Club. The club's interest in nautical matters is well known and it is always looking forward to the day when it will be able to command a vessel of its own. Now it would be too much to say that the club expected to be able to buy the *Hauppauge* (the first thing it would have done, in that case, would have been to rename her). For it was in the slack and hollow of the week—shall we

say, the bight of the week?—just midway between pay-
days. But at any rate, thought the club, we can look
her over, which will be an adventure in itself; and we
can see just how people behave when they are buying a
schooner, and how prices are running, so that when the
time comes we will be more experienced. Besides, the
club remembered the ship auction scene in "The
Wrecker" and felt that the occasion might be one of
most romantic excitement.

It is hard, it is very hard, to have to admit that the
club was foiled. It had been told that at Cortlandt
Street a ferry bound for Weehawken might be found;
but when Endymion and the Secretary arrived there,
at 12:20 o'clock, they learned that the traffic to Weehawken is somewhat sparse. Next boat at 2:40, said a
sign. They hastened to the Lackawanna ferry at Barclay Street, thinking that by voyaging to Hoboken and
then taking a car they might still be in time. But it
was not to be. When the *Ithaca* docked, just south of
the huge red-blotched profile of the rusty rotting
Leviathan, it was already 1 o'clock. The *Hauppauge*,
they said to themselves, is already on the block, and if
we went up there now to study her, we would be regarded
as impostors.

But the club is philosophic. One Adventure is very
nearly as good as another, and they trod ashore at
Hoboken with light hearts. It was a day of tender and
untroubled sunshine. They had a queer sensation of
being in foreign lands. Indeed, the tall tragic funnels
of the *Leviathan* and her motionless derelict masts cast
a curious shadow of feeling over that region. For the

great ship, though blameless herself, seems a thing of shame, a remembrance of days and deeds that soiled the simple creed of the sea. Her great shape and her majestic hull, pitiably dingy and stark, are yet plainly conscious of sin. You see it in every line of her as she lies there, with the attitude of a great dog beaten and crouching. You wonder how she would behave if she were towed out on the open bright water of the river, under that clear sky, under the eyes of other ships going about their affairs with the self-conscious rectitude and pride that ships have. For ships are creatures of intense caste and self-conscious righteousness. They rarely forgive a fallen sister—even when she has fallen through no fault of her own. Observe the *Nieuw Amsterdam* as she lies, very solid and spick, a few piers above. Her funnel is gay with bright green stripes; her glazed promenade deck is white and immaculate. But, is there not just a faint suggestion of smugness in her mien? She seems thanking the good old Dutch Deity of cleanliness and respectability that she herself is not like this poor trolloping giantess, degraded from the embrace of ocean and the unblemished circle of the sea.

That section of Hoboken waterfront, along toward the green promontory crowned by Stevens Institute, still has a war-time flavour. The old Hamburg-American line piers are used by the Army Transport Service, and in the sunshine a number of soldiers, off duty, were happily drowsing on a row of two-tiered beds set outdoors in the April pleasantness. There was a racket of bugles, and a squad seemed to be drilling in the courtyard. Endymion and the Secretary, after sitting on a pier-end watching some barges, and airing their nautical views in a way they would never have done had any pukka seafaring men been along, were stricken with the very crisis of spring fever and lassitude. They considered the possibility of hiring one of the soldiers' two-tiered beds for the afternoon. Perhaps it is the first two syllables of Hoboken's name that make it so desperately debilitating to the wayfarer in an April noonshine. Perhaps it was a kind of old nostalgia, for the Secretary remembered that sailormen's street as it had been some years ago, when he had been along there in search of schooners of another sort.

But anatomizing their anguish, these creatures finally decided that it might not be spring fever, but merely hunger. They saw the statue of the late Mr. Sloan of the Lackawanna Railroad—Sam Sloan, the bronze calls him, with friendly familiarity. The aspiring forelock of that statue, and the upraised finger of Samuel Sullivan Cox ("The Letter Carriers' Friend") in Astor Place, the club considers two of the most striking things in New York statuary. Mr. Pappanicholas, who has a candy shop in the high-spirited building called Duke's House, near the ferry terminal, must be (Endymion thought) some relative of Santa Claus. Perhaps he *is* Santa Claus, and the club pondered on the quite new idea that Santa Claus has lived in Hoboken all these years and no one had guessed it. The club asked a friendly policeman if there were a second-hand bookstore anywhere near. "Not that I know of," he said. But they did find a stationery store where there were a number of popular reprints in the window, notably "The Innocence of Father Brown," and Andrew Lang's "My Own Fairy Book."

But lunch was still to be considered. The club is happy to add The American Hotel, Hoboken, to its private list of places where it has been serenely happy. Consider corned beef hash, with fried egg, excellent, for 25 cents. Consider rhubarb pie, quite adequate, for 10 cents. Consider the courteous and urbane waiter. In one corner of the dining room was the hotel office, with a large array of push buttons communicating with the bedrooms. The club, its imagination busy, conceived that these were for the purpose of awakening seafaring guests early in the morning, so as not to miss their ship. If we were, for instance, second mate of the *Hauppauge*, and came to port in Hoboken, The American Hotel would be just the place where we would want to put up.

That brings us back to the *Hauppauge*. We wonder who bought her, and how much he paid; and why she carries the odd name of that Long Island village? If he would only invite us over to see her—and tell us how to get there!

THE CLUB AT ITS WORST

A BARBECUE and burgoo of the Three Hours for Lunch Club was held, the club's medical adviser acting as burgoomaster and Mr. Lawton Mackall, the managing director, as jest of honour. The news that Lawton was at large spread rapidly through the city, and the club was trailed for some distance by an infuriated agent of the Society for the Deracination of Puns. But Lawton managed to kick over his traces, and the club safely gained the quiet haven of a Cedar Street chophouse. Here, when the members were duly squeezed into a stall, the Doctor gazed cheerfully upon Endymion and the Secretary who held the inward places. "Now is my chance," he cried, "to kill two bards with one stone."

Lawton, says the stenographic report, was in excellent form, and committed a good deal of unforgivable syntax. He was somewhat apprehensive when he saw the bill of fare inscribed "Ye Olde Chop House," for he asserts that the use of the word "Ye" always involves extra overhead expense—and a quotation from Shakespeare on the back of the menu, he doubted, might mean a couvert charge. But he was distinctly cheered when the kidneys and bacon arrived—a long strip of bacon gloriously balanced on four very spherical and well-lubricated kidneys. Smiling demurely, even blandly, Lawton rolled his sheave of bacon to and fro upon its kidneys. "This is the first time I ever saw bacon with ball bearings," he ejaculated. He gazed with the eye of a connoisseur upon the rather candid works of art hanging over the club's corner. He said they reminded him of Mr. Coles Phillips's calf-tones. The Doctor was speaking of having read an interesting dispatch by Mr. Grasty in the *Times*. "I understand," said Lawton, "that he is going to collect some of his articles in a book, to be called 'Leaves of Grasty'."

Duly ambered with strict and cloudy cider, the meal progressed, served with humorous comments by the waitress whom the club calls the Venus of Mealo. The motto of the club is *Tres Horas Non Numero Nisi Serenas*, and as the afternoon was still juvenile the gathering was transferred to the waterfront. Passing onto the pier, Lawton gazed about him with admirable naïveté. Among the piles of freight were some agricultural machines. "Ha," cried the managing director, "this, evidently, is where the Piers Plowman works!" The club's private yacht, white and lovely, lay at her berth, and in the Doctor's cabin the members proceeded to the serious discussion of literature. Lawton, however, seemed nervous. Cargo was being put aboard the ship, and ever and anon there rose a loud rumbling of donkey engines. The occasional hurrying roar of machinery seemed to make Lawton nervous, for he said apprehensively that he feared someone was rushing the growler. In the corridor outside the Doctor's quarters a group of stewardesses were violently altercating, and Lawton remarked that a wench can make almost as much noise as a winch. On the whole, however, he admired the ship greatly, and was taken with the club's plans for going cruising. He said he felt safer after noting that the lifeboats were guaranteed to hold forty persons with cubic feet.

By this time, all sense of verbal restraint had been lost, and the club (if we must be candid) concluded its session by chanting, not without enjoyment, its own sea chantey, which runs as follows:—

> I shipped aboard a galleass
>   In a brig whereof men brag,
> But lying on my palliass
>   My spirits began to sag.

> I heard the starboard steward
>   Singing abaft the poop;
> He lewdly sang to looard
>   And sleep fled from the sloop.

> "The grog slops over the fiddles
>   With the violins of the gale:
> Two bitts are on the quarterdeck,
>   The seamen grouse and quail.

Plum Pudding

"The anchor has been catted,
  The timid ratlines flee,
Careening and carousing
  She yaws upon the sea.

"The skipper lies in the scupper,
  The barque is lost in the bight;
The bosun calls for a basin—
  This is a terrible night.

"The wenches man the winches,
  The donkeymen all bray—"
  . . . I hankered to be anchored
  In safety in the bay!

A SUBURBAN SENTIMENTALIST

THAT wild and engaging region known as the Salamis Estates has surprising enchantments for the wanderer. Strolling bushrangers, if they escape being pelleted with lead by the enthusiastic rabbit hunters who bang suddenly among thickets, will find many vistas of loveliness. All summer long we are imprisoned in foliage, locked up in a leafy embrace. But when the leaves have shredded away and the solid barriers of green stand revealed as only thin fringes of easily penetrable woodland, the eye moves with surprise over these wide reaches of colour and freedom. Beyond the old ruined farmhouse past the gnarled and rheumatic apple tree is that dimpled path that runs across fields, the short cut down to the harbour. The stiff frozen plumes of ghostly goldenrod stand up pale and powdery along the way. How many tints of brown and fawn and buff in the withered grasses—some as feathery and translucent as a gauze scarf, as nebulous as those veilings Robin Herrick was so fond of—his mention of them gives an odd connotation to a modern reader—

[133]

Plum Pudding

So looks Anthea, when in bed she lyes,
Orecome, or halfe betray'd by Tiffanies.

Our fields now have the rich, tawny colour of a panther's
hide.   Along the little path are scattered sumac leaves,
dark scarlet. It is as though Summer had been
wounded by the hunter Jack Frost, and had crept away
down that secret track, leaving a trail of bloodstains behind her.

This tract of placid and enchanted woodland, field,
brake, glen, and coppice, has always seemed to us so
amazingly like the magical Forest of Arden that we believe Shakespeare must have written "As You Like It"
somewhere near here.   One visitor, who was here when
the woods were whispering blackly in autumn moonlight, thought them akin to George Meredith's "The
Woods of Westermain"—

> Enter these enchanted woods,
>   You who dare.
> Nothing harms beneath the leaves
> More than waves a swimmer cleaves.
> Toss your heart up with the lark,
> Foot at peace with mouse and worm.
>   Fair you fare.
> Only at a dread of dark
> Quaver, and they quit their form:
> Thousand eyeballs under hoods
>   Have you by the hair.
> Enter these enchanted woods,
>   You who dare.

But in winter, and in such a noonday of clear sunshine
as the present, when all the naked grace of trunks and

hillsides lies open to eyeshot, the woodland has less of that secrecy and brooding horror that Meredith found in "Westermain." It has the very breath of that golden-bathed magic that moved in Shakespeare's tenderest haunt of comedy. Momently, looking out toward the gray ruin on the hill (which was once, most likely, the very "sheepcote fenced about with olive trees" where Aliena dwelt and Ganymede found hose and doublet give such pleasing freedom to her limbs and her wit) one expects to hear the merry note of a horn; the moralizing Duke would come striding thoughtfully through the thicket down by the tiny pool (or shall we call it a mere?). He would sit under those two knotty old oaks and begin to pluck the burrs from his jerkin. Then would come his cheerful tanned followers, carrying the dappled burgher they had ambushed; and, last, the pensive Jacques (so very like Mr. Joseph Pennell in bearing and humour) distilling his meridian melancholy into pentameter paragraphs, like any colyumist. A bonfire is quickly kindled, and the hiss and fume of venison collops whiff to us across the blue air. Against that stump—is it a real stump, or only a painted canvas affair from the property man's warehouse?—surely that is a demijohn of cider? And we can hear, presently, that most piercingly tremulous of all songs rising in rich chorus, with the plenitude of pathos that masculines best compass after a full meal—

> Blow, blow, thou winter wind,
> Thou art not so unkind
> As man's ingratitude—

Plum Pudding

We hum the air over to ourself, and are stricken with the most perfect iridescent sorrow. We even ransack our memory to try to think of someone who has been ungrateful to us, so that we can throw a little vigorous bitterness into our tone.

Yes, the sunshine that gilds our Salamis thickets seems to us to have very much the amber glow of footlights.

In another part of this our "forest"—it is so truly a forest in the Shakespearean sense, as all Long Island forests are (e. g., Forest Hills), where even the lioness and the green and gilded snake have their suburban analogues, which we will not be laborious to explain—we see Time standing still while Ganymede and Aliena are out foraging with the burly Touchstone (so very like that well-loved sage Mr. Don Marquis, we protest!). And, to consider, what a place for a colyumist was the Forest of Arden. See how zealous contributors hung their poems round on trees so that he could not miss them. Is it not all the very core and heartbeat of what we call "romance," that endearing convention that submits the harsh realities and interruptions of life to a golden purge of fancy? How, we sometimes wonder, can any one grow old as long as he can still read "As You Like It," and feel the magic of that best-loved and most magical of stage directions—*The Forest of Arden*.

And now, while we are still in the soft Shakespearean mood, comes "Twelfth Night"—traditionally devoted to dismantling the Christmas Tree; and indeed there is no task so replete with luxurious and gentle melancholy. For by that time the toys which erst were so splendid are battered and bashed; the cornucopias empty of candy (save one or two striped sticky shards of peppermint which elude the thrusting index, and will be found again next December); the dining-room floor is thick with fallen needles; the gay little candles are burnt down to a small gutter of wax in the tin holders. The floor sparkles here and there with the fragments of tinsel balls or popcorn chains that were injudiciously hung within leap of puppy or grasp of urchin. And so you see him, the diligent parent, brooding with a tender mournfulness and sniffing the faint whiff of that fine Christmas tree odour—balsam and burning candles and fist-warmed peppermint—as he undresses the prickly boughs. Here they go into the boxes, red, green, and golden balls, tinkling glass bells, stars, paper angels, cotton-wool Santa Claus, blue birds, celluloid goldfish, mosquito netting, counterfeit stockings, nickel-plated horns, and all the comical accumulation of oddities that gathers from year to year in the box labelled CHRISTMAS TREE THINGS, FRAGILE. The box goes up to the attic, and the parent blows a faint diminuendo, achingly prolonged, on a toy horn. Titania is almost reduced to tears as he explains it is the halloo of Santa Claus fading away into the distance.

GISSING

OUR subject, for the moment, is Gissing—and when we say Gissing we mean not the author of that name, but the dog. He was called Gissing because he arrived, in the furnace man's poke, on the same day on which, after long desideration, we were united in holy booklock with a copy of "By the Ionian Sea."

Gissing needs (as the man said who wrote the preface to Sir Kenelm Digby's *Closet*) no Rhetoricating Floscules to set him off. He is (as the man said who wrote a poem about New York) vulgar of manner, underbred. He is young: his behaviour lacks restraint. Yet there is in him some lively prescription of that innocent and indivisible virtue that Nature omitted from men and gave only to Dogs. This is something that has been the cause of much vile verse in bad poets, of such gruesome twaddle as Senator Vest's dreadful outbark. But it is a true thing.

How absurd, we will interject, is the saying: "Love me, love my dog." If he really is my dog, he won't let you

[138]

love him. Again, one man's dog is another man's mongrel. Mr. Robert Cortes Holliday, that quaint philosopher frequently doggishly nicknamed Owd Bob, went to Washington lately to see President Harding. His eye fell upon the White House Airedale. Now Owd Bob is himself something of an Airedale trifler, and cherishes the memory of a certain Tristram Shandy, an animal that frequently appeared in the lighter editorials of the *Bookman* when Mr. Holliday (then the editor) could think of nothing else to write about. And of Mr. Harding's dog Mr. Holliday reports, with grave sorrow: "I don't think he is a good Airedale. He has too much black on him. Now Shandy had only a small saddle of black. . . ."

But such are matters concerning only students of full-bred dogs, of whom we are not who.

As to Gissing: we were trying to think, while writing the preceding excursion, how to give you his colour. Yellow is a word too violent, too vulgarly connotative. Brown is a muddy word. Sandy is too pale. Gamboge is a word used by artists, who are often immoral and excitable. Shall we say, the colour of a corncob pipe, singed and tawnied by much smoking? Or a pigskin tobacco pouch while it is still rather new? Or the colour of the *Atlantic Monthly* in the old days, when it lay longer on the stands than it does now, and got faintly bleached? And in this colour, whatever it is, you must discern a dimly ruddy tinge. On his forehead, which is not really a forehead, but a continuation of a long and very vulpine nose, there is a small white stripe. It runs upward from between his eyes, but cants slightly to one side (like a great many journalists). There is a small white patch on his chin. There is a white waistcoat on his chest, or bosom if you consider that a more affectionate word. White also are the last twelve bristles (we have counted them) on his tail (which is much too long). His front ankles bend inward rather lopsidedly, as though he had fallen downstairs when very young. When we stoke the furnace, he extends his forward legs on the floor (standing erect the while in his rearward edifice) and lays his head sideways on his paws, and considers us in a manner not devoid of humour.

Not far from our house, in that desirable but not very residential region which we have erst described as the Forest of Arden, there is a pond. It is a very romantic spot, it is not unlike the pond by which a man smoking a Trichinopoly cigar was murdered in one of the Sherlock Holmes stories. (The Boscombe Valley Mystery!) It is a shallow little pond, but the water is very clear; last winter when it was frozen it always reminded us of the cheerful advertising of one of the ice companies, it was so delightfully transparent. This pond is a kind of Union League Club for the frogs at this time of year; all night long you can hear them reclining in their armchairs of congenial mud and uttering their opinions, which vary very little from generation to generation. Most of those frogs are Republicans, we feel sure, but we love them no less.

In this pond Gissing had his first swim one warm Sunday recently. The party set out soon after breakfast. Gissing was in the van, his topaz eyes wild with ambition. Followed a little red express-wagon, in which sat the Urchiness, wearing her best furry hat which has, in front, a small imitation mouse-head with glass eyes. The Urchin, wearing a small Scotch bonnet with ribbons, assisted in hauling the wagon. Gissing had not yet been tested in the matter of swimming: this was a sober moment. Would he take gladly to the ocean? (So the Urchin innocently calls our small sheet of water, having by a harmless ratiocination concluded that this term applies to any body of water not surrounded by domestic porcelain.)

Now Gissing is passionate in the matter of chasing sticks hurled abroad. On seeing a billet seized and held aloft with that sibilant sound which stirs his ingenuous spirit to prodigies of pursuit, his eyes were flame, his heart was apoplexy. The stick flew aloft and curved into the pond, and he rushed to the water's edge. But there, like the recreant knight in the Arthurian idyl, he paused and doubted. There was Excalibur, floating ten feet from shore. This was a new experience. Was it written that sticks should be pursued in this strange and alien element? He barked querulously, and returned, his intellect clouded with hesitation. What was this etiquette? He was embarrassed.

Another stick was flung into the trembling mere. This time there was no question. When the gods give the same sign twice, the only answer is obey. A tawny streak crossed the small meadow, and leaped unquestioningly into the pond. There was a plunging and a spattery scuffle, and borne up by a million years of heredity he pursued the floating enemy. It was seized, and a large gulp of water also, but backward he came bearing it merrily. Then, also unknowing that he was fulfilling old tradition, he came as near as possible to the little group of presbyters and dehydrated himself upon them. Thus was a new experience added to this young creature. The frogs grew more and more pensive as he spent the rest of the morning churning the pond hither and thither.

That will be all about Gissing for the present.

A DIALOGUE

IT WAS our good fortune to overhear a dialogue between Gissing (our dog) and Mike, the dog who lives next door. Mike, or Crowgill Mike II, to give him his full entitles, is a very sagacious old person, in the fifteenth year of his disillusionment, and of excellent family. If our humble Gissing is to have a three-barrelled name, it can only be Haphazard Gissing I, for his ancestry is plainly miscellaneous and impromptu. He is, we like to say, a synthetic dog. He is young: six months; we fear that some of the errors now frequently urged against the rising generation are plainly discernible in him. And Mike, who is grizzled and grown somewhat dour, shows toward our Gissing much the attitude of Dr. Eliot toward the younger litter of humans.

In public, and when any one is watching, Mike, who is the Dog Emeritus of the Salamis Estates, pays no heed to Gissing at all: ignores him, and prowls austerely about his elderly business. But secretly spying from a window, we have seen him, unaware of notice, stroll (a little heavily and stiffly, for an old dog's legs grow gouty) over to Gissing's kennel. With his tail slightly vibrant, he conducts a dignified causerie. Unhappily, these talks are always concluded by some breach of manners on Gissing's part. At first he is respectful; but presently his enthusiasm grows too much for him; he begins to leap and frolic and utter uncouth praises of things in general. Then Mike turns soberly and moves away.

On such an occasion, the chat went like this:

GISSING: Do you believe in God?

MIKE: I acknowledge Him. I don't believe in Him.

GISSING: Oh, I think He's splendid. Hurrah! Hullabaloo! When He puts on those old khaki trousers and smokes that curve-stem pipe I always know there's a good time coming.

MIKE: You have made a mistake. That is not God. God is a tall, placid, slender man, who wears puttees when He works in the garden and smokes only cigarettes.

GISSING: Not at all. God is quite stout, and of uncertain temper, but I adore Him.

MIKE: No one knows God at your age. There is but one God, and I have described Him. There is no doubt about it, because He sometimes stays away from the office on Saturdays. Only God can do that.

GISSING: What a glorious day this is. What ho! Halleluiah! I don't suppose you know what fun it is to run round in circles. How ignorant of life the older generation is.

A Dialogue

MIKE: Humph.

GISSING: Do you believe in Right and Wrong? I mean, are they absolute, or only relative?

MIKE: When I was in my prime Right was Right, and Wrong was Wrong. A bone, buried on someone else's ground, was sacred. I would not have dreamed of digging it up——

GISSING (*hastily*): But I am genuinely puzzled. Suppose a motor truck goes down the road. My instinct tells me that I ought to chase it and bark loudly. But if God is around He calls me back and rebukes me, sometimes painfully. Yet I am convinced that there is nothing essentially wrong in my action.

MIKE: The question of morals is not involved. If you were not so young and foolish you would know that your God (if you so call Him, though He is not a patch on mine) knows what is good for you better than you do yourself. He forbids your chasing cars because you might get hurt.

GISSING: Then instinct is not to be obeyed?

MIKE: Not when God is around.

GISSING: Yet He encourages me to chase sticks, which my instinct strongly impels me to do. Prosit! Waes hael! Excuse my enthusiasm, but you really know very little of the world or you would not take things so calmly.

MIKE: My dear boy, rheumatism is a great sedative. You will learn by and by. What are you making such a racket about?

GISSING: I have just learned that there is no such thing as free will. I don't suppose you ever meditated

on these things, you are such an old stick-in-the-mud.
But in my generation we scrutinize everything.

MIKE: There is plenty of free will when you have
learned to will the right things. But there's no use
willing yourself to destroy a motor truck, because it
can't be done. I have been young, and now am old,
but never have I seen an honest dog homeless, nor his
pups begging their bones. You will go to the devil if
you don't learn to restrain yourself.

GISSING: Last night there was a white cat in the
sky. Yoicks, yoicks! I ran thirty times round the
house, yelling.

MIKE: Only the moon, nothing to bark about.

GISSING: You are very old, and I do not think you
have ever really felt the excitement of life. Excuse me,
but have you seen me jump up and pull the baby's
clothes from the line? It is glorious fun.

MIKE: My good lad, I think life will deal hardly
with you.

(*Exit, shaking his head.*)

AT THE GASTHOF ZUM OCHSEN

LOOKING over some several-days-old papers we observe that the truant Mr. Bergdoll was discovered at Eberbach in Baden. Well, well, we meditate, Herr Bergdoll is not wholly devoid of sense, if he is rambling about that delicious valley of the Neckar. And if we were a foreign correspondent, anxious to send home to the papers a complete story of Herr Bergdoll's doings in those parts, we would know exactly what to do. We would go straight to the excellent Herr Leutz, proprietor of the *Gasthof zum Ochsen* in Eberbach, and listen to his prattle. Herr Leutz, whom we have never forgotten (since we once spent a night in his inn, companioned by another vagabond who is now Prof. W. L. G. Williams of Cornell University, so our clients in Ithaca, if any, can check us up on this fact), is the most innocently talkative person we have ever met.

A great many Americans have been to Alt Heidelberg, but not so many have continued their exploration up the Neckarthal. You leave Heidelberg by the Philosophers' Way (*Philosophenweg*), which looks over the river and the hills—in this case, lit by a warm July sunset—and follow (on your bicycle, of course) the road which skirts the stream. There are many springs of cold water tinkling down the steep banks on your left, and in the mediæval-looking village of Hirschhorn you can also sample the excellent beer. The evening smell of sun-warmed grass and a view of one of those odd boats grinding its way up-current by hauling a chain from the river-bed and dropping it again over-stern will do nothing to mar your exhilaration. It will be getting dark when you reach Eberbach, and if you find your way to the Ox, Herr Leutz will be waiting (we hope) in his white coat and gold pince-nez, just as he was in 1912. And then, as you sit down to a cold supper, he will, deliberately and in the kindest way, proceed to talk your head off. He will sit down with you at the table, and every time you think a pause is coming he will seize a mug, rise to his feet (at which you also will sadly lay down your tools and rise, too, bowing stiffly from your hips), and cry: "*Also! ich trinke auf Ihr Wohl!*" Presently, becoming more assured, the admirable creature abbreviates his formula to the more companionable "*zum Wohl!*" And as he talks, and his excitement becomes more and more intense, he edges closer and closer to you, and leans forward, talking hard, until his dark beaming phiz quite interposes between your food and its destination. So that to avoid combing his baldish pate with your fork you must pass the items of your meal in quite a sideways trajectory. And if, as happened to our companion (the present Cornell don), you have no special taste for a plump landlord breathing passionately and genially upon your very cheek while you strive to satisfy a legitimate appetite, you may burst into a sudden unpremeditate but uncontrollable screech of mingled laughter and dismay, meanwhile almost falling backward in your chair in an effort to evade the steady pant and roar of those innumerable gutturals.

After supper, a little weary and eager to meditate calmly in the delicious clear evening, and to look about and see what sort of place this Eberbach is, you will slip outside the inn for a stroll. But glorious Herr Leutz is not evadable. He comes with. He takes position between you two, holding each firmly by an elbow so that no escape is possible. In a terrific stream of friendliness he explains everything, particularly expatiating upon the gratification he feels at being honoured by visitors all the way from America. The hills around, which stand up darkly against a speckle of stars, are all discussed for you. One of them is called *Katzenbuckel*, and doubting that your German may not be able to cope with this quite simple compound, he proceeds to illustrate. He squats in the middle of the street, arching his back like a cat in a strong emotion, uttering lively miaowings and hissings. Then he springs, like the feline in fury, and leaps to his feet roaring with mirth. "You see?" he cries. "A cat, who all ready to spring crouches, that is of our beautiful little mountain the name-likeness."

Yes, if Bergdoll has been staying in Eberbach, the good Herr Leutz will know all about it.

MR CONRAD'S NEW PREFACE

JOSEPH CONRAD, so we learn from the March *Bookman*, has written a preface to a cook book about to be published by Mrs. Conrad.

We like to think about that preface. We wonder if it will be anything like this:

I remember very well the first time I became aware of the deep and consoling significance of food. It was one evening at Marlow's, we were sitting by the hearth in that small gilded circle of firelight that seems so like the pitiful consciousness of man, temporarily and gallantly relieved against the all-covering darkness. Marlow was in his usual posture, cross-legged on the rug. He was talking. . . . I couldn't help wondering whether he ever gets pins and needles in his legs, sitting so long in one position. Very often, you know, what

Plum Pudding

those Eastern visionaries mistake for the authentic visit of Ghautama Buddha is merely pins and needles. However. Humph. Poor Mrs. Marlow (have I mentioned her before?) was sitting somewhere in the rear of the circle. I had a curious but quite distinct impression that she wanted to say something, that she had, as people say, something on her mind. But Marlow has a way of casting pregnancy over even his pauses, so that to speak would seem a quite unpardonable interruption.

"The power of mind over matter," said Marlow, suddenly, "a very odd speculation. When I was on the *Soliloquy*, I remember one evening, in the fiery serenity of a Sourabaja sunset, there was an old serang . . ."

In the ample drawing room, lit only by those flickering gleams of firelight, I seemed to see the others stir faintly—not so much a physical stir as a half-divined spiritual uneasiness. The Director was sitting too close to the glow, for the fire had deepened and intensified as the great logs slowly burned into rosy embers, and I could smell a whiff of scorching trouser legs; but the courageous man dared not move, for fear of breaking the spell. Marlow's tale was a powerful one: I could hear Mrs. Marlow suspire faintly, ever so faintly—the troubled, small, soft sigh of a brave woman indefinably stricken. The gallantry of women! In a remote part of the house a ship's clock tingled its quick double strokes. . . . Eight o'clock, I thought, unconsciously translating nautical horology into the dull measurements of landsmen. None of us moved. The discipline of the sea!

Mr. Conrad's New Preface

Mrs. Marlow was very pale. It began to come over me that there was an alien presence, something spectral and immanent, something empty and yet compelling, in the mysterious shadow and vagueness of the chamber. More than once, as Marlow had coasted us along those shining seascapes of Malaya—we had set sail from Malacca at tea time, and had now got as far as Batu Beru— I had had an uneasy impression that a disturbed white figure had glanced pallidly through the curtains, had made a dim gesture, and had vanished again. . . . I had tried to concentrate on Marlow's narrative. The dear fellow looked more like a monkey than ever, squatting there, as he took the *Soliloquy* across the China Sea and up the coast of Surinam. Surinam must have a very long coast-line, I was thinking. But perhaps it was that typhoon that delayed us. . . . Really, he ought not to make his descriptions so graphic, for Mrs. Marlow, I feared, was a bad sailor, and she was beginning to look quite ill. . . . I caught her looking over her shoulder in a frightened shudder, as though seeking the companionway.

It was quite true. By the time we had reached Tonking, I felt sure there was someone else in the room. In my agitation I stole a cautious glance from the taffrail of my eye and saw a white figure standing hesitantly by the door, in an appalled and embarrassed silence. The Director saw it, too, for he was leaning as far away from the fire as he could without jibing his chair, and through the delicate haze of roasting tweed that surrounded him I could see something wistfully appealing in his glance. The Lawyer, too, had a mysterious shimmer in his loyal eyes, but his old training in the P. and O. service had been too strong for him. He would never speak, I felt sure, while his commanding officer had the floor.

I began to realize that, in a sense, the responsibility was mine. The life of the sea—a curious contradiction. Trained from boyhood to assume responsibility, but responsibility graded and duly ascending through the ranks of command. Marlow, an old shipmaster, and more than that, our host—a trying problem. If it had not been for the presence of Mrs. Marlow, I could not have dared. But the woman complicates the situation with all sorts of delicate reactions of tact, conduct, and necessity. It is always so. Well. Humph!

But the apparition at the other end of the room was plainly in trouble. A distressing sight, and I divined that the others were relying on me. Mrs. Marlow, poor soul, her face had a piteous and luminous appeal. It was, once more, the old and shocking question of conflicting loyalties. There was nothing else to do. I shoved out one foot, and the stand of fire-irons fell over with an appalling clatter. Marlow broke off—somewhere near Manila, I think it was.

"Charlie, my dear," said Mrs. Marlow, "Don't you think we could finish the story after dinner? The roast will be quite spoiled. The maid has been waiting for nearly two hours. . . ."

THE LITTLE HOUSE

AFTER many days of damp, dull, and dolorous weather, we found ourself unexpectedly moving in a fresh, cool, pure air; an air which, although there was no sunlight, had the spirit and feeling of sunlight in it; an air which was purged and lively. And, so strangely do things happen, after days of various complexion and stratagem, we found ourself looking across that green field, still unchanged, at the little house.

Wasn't there—we faintly recall a saccharine tune sung by someone who strode stiffly to and fro in a glare of amber footlights—wasn't there a song about: "And I lo-ong to settle down, in that old Long Island town!" Wasn't there such a ditty? It came softly back, unbidden, to the sentimental attic of our memory as we passed along that fine avenue of trees and revisited, for the first time since we moved away, the wide space of those Long Island fields and the row of frame cottages. There was the little house, rather more spick and span than when we had known it, freshly painted in its brown and white, the privet hedge very handsomely shaven, and its present occupant busily engaged in trimming some tufts of grass along the pavement. We did not linger, and that cheerful-looking man little knew how many ghosts he was living among. All of us, we suppose, dwell amid ghosts we are not aware of, and this gentleman would be startled if he knew the tenacity and assurance of certain shades who moved across his small lawn that afternoon.

It was strange, we aver, to see how little the place had changed, for it seemed that we had passed round the curves and contours of a good many centuries in those four or five years. In the open meadow the cow was still grazing; perhaps the same cow that was once pestered by a volatile Irish terrier who used to swing merrily at the end of that cow's tail; a merry and irresponsible little creature, she was, and her phantom still scampers the road where the sharp scream of the Freeport trolley brings back her last fatal venture to our mind. It was strange to look at those windows, with their neat white sills, and to remember how we felt when for the first time we slept in a house of our own, with all those Long Island stars crowding up to the open window, and, waking in drowsy unbelief, put out a hand to touch the strong wall and see if it was still there. Perhaps one may be pardoned for being a little sentimental in thinking back about one's first house.

The Little House

The air, on that surprising afternoon, carried us again into the very sensation and reality of those days, for there is an openness and breezy stir on those plains that is characteristic. In the tree-lined streets of the village, where old white clapboarded houses with green or pale blue shutters stand in a warm breath of box hedges, the feeling is qu'te different. Out on the Long Island prairie—which Walt Whitman, by the way, was one of the first to love and praise—you stand uncovered to all the skirmish of heaven, and the feathery grasses are rarely still. There was the chimney of the fireplace we had built for us, and we remembered how the wood-smoke used to pour gallantly from it like a blue pennon of defiance. The present owner, we fear, does not know how much impalpable and unforgotten gold leaped up the wide red throat of that chimney, or he would not dream of selling. Yes, the neighbours tell us that he wants to sell. In our day, the house was said to be worth $3,000. Nowadays, the price is $7,000. Even at that it is cheap, if you set any value on amiable and faithful ghosts.

Oh, little house on the plains, when our typewriter forgets thee, may this shift key lose its function!

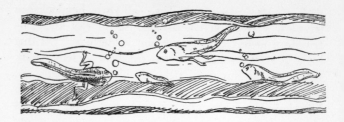

TADPOLES

NEAR our house, out in the sylvan Salamis Estates, there is a pond. We fear we cannot describe this pond to you in a way to carry conviction. You will think we exaggerate if we tell you, with honest warmth, how fair the prospect is. Therefore, in sketching the scene, we will be austere, churlish, a miser of adjectives. We will tell you naught of sun-sparkle by day where the green and gold of April linger in that small hollow landskip, where the light shines red through the faint bronze veins of young leaves—much as it shines red through the finger joinings of a child's hand held toward the sun. We will tell you naught of frog-song by night, of those reduplicated whistlings and peepings. We will tell you naught of. . . . No, we will be austere.

On one side, this pond reflects the white cloudy bravery of fruit trees in flower, veterans of an orchard surviving an old farmhouse that stood on the hilltop long ago. It burned, we believe: only a rectangle of low stone walls remains. Opposite, the hollow is overlooked by a bumpy hillock fringed with those excellent

Tadpoles

dark evergreen trees—shall we call them hemlocks?—
whose flat fronds silhouette against the sky and con-
tribute a feeling of mystery and wilderness. On this
little hill are several japonica trees, in violent ruddy
blossom; and clumps of tiger lily blades springing up;
and bloodroots. The region prickles thickly with
blackberry brambles, and mats of honeysuckle. Across
the pond, looking from the waterside meadow where
the first violets are, your gaze skips (like a flat stone
deftly flung) from the level amber (dimpled with
silver) of the water, through a convenient dip of country
where the fields are folded down below the level of the
pool. So the eye, skittering across the water, leaps
promptly and cleanly to blue ranges by the Sound, a
couple of miles away. All this, mere introduction to
the real theme, which is Tadpoles.

We intended to write a poem about those tadpoles,
but Endymion tells us that Louis Untermeyer has already smitten a lute on that topic. We are queasy of
trailing such an able poet. Therefore we celebrate
these tadpoles in prose. They deserve a prose as lucid,
as limpid, as cool and embracing, as the water of their
home.

Coming back to tadpoles, the friends of our youth,
shows us that we have completed a biological cycle of
much import. Back to tadpoles in one generation, as
the adage might have said. Twenty-five years ago
we ourself were making our first acquaintance with
these friendly creatures, in the immortal (for us) waters
of Cobb's Creek, Pennsylvania. (Who was Cobb, we
wonder?) And now our urchins, with furious glee,

applaud their sire who wades the still frosty quags of our pond, on Sunday mornings, to renew their supply of tads. It is considered fair and decent that each batch of tadpoles should live in their prison (a milk bottle) only one week. The following Sunday they go back to the pond, and a new generation take their places. There is some subtle kinship, we think, between children and tadpoles. No childhood is complete until it has watched their sloomy and impassive faces munching against the glass, and seen the gradual egress (as the encyclopædia pedantically puts it) of their tender limbs, the growing froggishness of their demeanour.

Some time when you are exploring in the Britannica, by the way, after you have read about Tactics and William Howard Taft, turn to the article on Tadpoles and see if you can recognize them as described by the learned G. A. B. An amusing game, we submit, would be to take a number of encyclopædia descriptions of familiar things, and see how many of our friends could identify them under their scientific nomenclature.

But it is very pleasant to dally about the pond on a mild April morning. While the Urchiness mutters among the violets, picking blue fistfuls of stalkless heads, the Urchin, on a plank at the waterside, studies these weedy shallows which are lively with all manner of mysterious excitement, and probes a waterlogged stump in hope to recapture Brer Tarrypin, who once was ours for a short while. Gissing (the juvenile and too enthusiastic dog) has to be kept away from the pond by repeated sticks thrown as far as possible in another direction; otherwise he insists on joining the tadpole search,

Tadpoles

and, poking his snout under water, attempts to bark at the same time, with much coughing and smother.

The tadpoles, once caught, are taken home in a small yellow pail. They seem quite cheerful. They are kept, of course, in their native fluid, which is liberally thickened with the oozy emulsion of moss, mud, and busy animalculæ that were dredged up with them in clutches along the bottom of the pond. They lie, thoughtful, at the bottom of their milk bottle, occasionally flourishing furiously round their prison. But, since reading that article in the Britannica, we are more tender toward them. For the learned G. A. B. says: "A glandular streak extending from the nostril toward the eye is the lachrymal canal." Is it possible that tadpoles weep? We will look at them again when we go home to-night. We are, in the main, a kind-hearted host. If they show any signs of effusion. . . .

MAGIC IN SALAMIS

WHY is it (we were wondering, as we walked to the station) that these nights of pearly wet Long Island fog make the spiders so active? The sun was trying to break through the mist, and all the way down the road trees, bushes, and grass were spangled with cobwebs, shining with tiny pricks and gems of moisture. These damp, mildewy nights that irritate us and bring that queer soft grayish fur on the backs of our books seem to mean high hilarity and big business to the spider. Along the hedge near the station there were wonderful great webs, as big as the shield of Achilles. What a surprising passion of engineering the spider must go through in the dark hours, to get his struts and cantilevers and his circling gossamer girders properly disposed on the foliage.* Darkness is no difficulty to

* Perhaps the structural talent of our Salamis arachnids is exceptional. Perhaps it is due to the fact that the famous Engineers' Country Club is near by. Can the spiders have learned their technology by watching those cheerful scientists on the golf greens?

him, evidently. If he lays his web on the grass, he builds it with a little tunnel leading down to earth, where he hides waiting his breakfast. But on such a morning, apparently, with thousands of webs ready, there can hardly have been enough flies to go round; for we saw all the appetent spiders had emerged from their tubes and were waiting impatiently on the web itself—as though the host should sit on the table-cloth waiting for his guest. Put a finger at the rim of the web and see how quickly he vanishes down his shaft. Most surprising of all it is to see the long threads that are flung horizontally through the air, from a low branch of a tree to the near-by hedge. They hang, elastic and perfect, sagged a little by a run of fog-drops almost invisible except where the wetness catches the light. Some were stretched at least six feet across space, with no supporting strands to hold them from above—and no branches from which the filament could be dropped. How is it done? Does our intrepid weaver hurl himself madly six feet into the dark, trusting to catch the leaf at the other end? Can he jump so far?

All this sort of thing is, quite plainly, magic. It is rather important to know, when you are dealing with magic, just where ordinary life ends and the mystery begins, so that you can adjust yourself to incantations and spells. As you make your green escape from town (which has magic of its own, but quite different) you must clearly mark the place where you pierce the veil. We showed it to Endymion lately. We will tell you about it.

Plum Pudding

There is a certain point, as you go out to Salamis on the railroad, when you begin to perceive a breath of enchantment in the landscape. For our own part, we become aware of a subtle spice of gramarye as soon as we see the station lamps at East Williston, which have tops like little green hats. Lamps of this sort have always had a fascination for us, and whenever we see them at a railway station we have a feeling that that would be a nice place to get off and explore.

And, of course, after you pass East Williston there is that little pond in which, if one went fishing, he could very likely pull up a fine fleecy cloud on his hook. Then the hills begin, or what we on Long Island consider hills. There are some fields on the left of the train that roll like great green waves of the sea; they surge up against the sky and seem about to spill over in a surf of daisies.

A quiet road runs up a hill, and as soon as you pass along its green channel, between rising thickets where rabbits come out to gape, you feel as though walking into a poem by Walter de la Mare. This road, if pursued, passes by a pleasing spot where four ways cross in an attenuated **X**. Off to one side is a field that is very theatrical in effect: it always reminds us of a stage set for "As You Like It," the Forest of Arden. There are some gigantic oak trees and even some very papier-maché-looking stumps, all ready for the duke, "and other Lords, like Foresters," to do their moralizing upon; and in place of the poor sequestered stag there is a very fine plushy cow, grazing, hard by a very agreeable morass. At the back (*L. U. E.*) is discovered a pleasing ruin, the carcass of an ancient farmstead, whose stony ribs are thickset with brambles; and the pleasant melancholy of an abandoned orchard rounds off the scene in the wings, giving a fine place for Rosalind and Celia and the leg-weary Touchstone to abide their cue.

Choosing the left-hand arm of the **X**, and moving past wild rose bushes toward the even richer rose-garden of the sunset, the fastidious truant is ushered (as was our friend Endymion the other evening) upon a gentle meadow where a solitary house of white stucco begs for a poet as occupant. This house, having been selected by Titania and ourself as a proper abode for Endymion and his family, we waited until sunset, frogsong, and all the other amenities of life in Salamis were suitable for the introduction of our guest to the scene. This dwelling, having long lain untenanted, has a back door that stands ajar and we piloted the awe-struck lyrist inside. Now nothing rages so merrily in the blood as the instinct of picking out houses for other people, houses that you yourself do not have to live in; and those Realtors whom we have dismayed by our lack of enthusiasm would have been startled to hear the orotund accents in which we vouched for that property, sewage, messuage, and all. Here, we cried, is the front door (facing the sunset) where the postman will call with checks from your publishers; and here are the porcelain laundry tubs that will make glad the heart of the washerwoman (when you can get one).

Endymion's guileless heart was strongly uplifted. Not a question did he ask as to heating arrangements, save to show a mild spark in his eye when he saw the two fireplaces. Plumbing was to him, we saw, a matter to be taken on faith. His paternal heart was slightly perturbed by a railing that ran round the top of the stairs. This railing, he feared, was so built that small and impetuous children would assuredly fall headlong through it, and we discussed means of thwarting such catastrophe. But upstairs we found the room that caused our guest to glimmer with innocent cheer. It had tall casement windows looking out upon a quiet glimpse of trees. It had a raised recess, very apt for a bust of Pallas. It had space for bookcases. And then, on the windowsill, we found the dead and desiccated corpse of a swallow. It must have flown in through a broken pane on the ground floor long ago and swooped vainly about the empty house. It lay, pathetically, close against the shut pane. Like a forgotten and un-uttered beauty in the mind of a poet, it lay there, stiffened and silent.

CONSIDER THE COMMUTER

WHEN they tell us the world is getting worse and worse, and the follies and peevishness of men will soon bring us all to some damnable perdition, we are consoled by contemplating the steadfast virtue of commuters. The planet grows harder and harder to live on, it is true; every new invention makes things more complicated and perplexing. These new automatic telephones, which are said to make the business of getting a number so easy, will mean (we suppose) that we will be called up fifty times a day—instead of (as now) a mere twenty or thirty, while we are swooning and swinking over a sonnet. But more and more people are taking to commuting and we look to that to save things.

Plum Pudding

Because commuting is a tough and gruelling discipline. It educes all the latent strength and virtue in a man (although it is hard on those at home, for when he wins back at supper time there is left in him very little of what the ladies so quaintly call "soul"). If you study the demeanour of fellow-passengers on the 8:04 and the 5:27 you will see a quiet and well-drilled acceptiveness, a pious non-resistance, which is not unworthy of the antique Chinese sages.

Is there any ritual (we cry, warming to our theme) so apt to imbue the spirit with patience, stolidity, endurance, all the ripe and seasoned qualities of manhood? It is well known that the fiercest and most terrible fighters in the late war were those who had been commuters. It was a Division composed chiefly of commuters that stormed the Hindenburg Stellung and purged the Argonne thickets with flame and steel. Their commanding officers were wont to remark these men's carelessness of life. It seemed as though they hardly heeded whether they got home again or not.

See them as they stand mobbed at the train gate, waiting for admission to the homeward cars. A certain disingenuous casualness appears on those hardened brows; but beneath burn stubborn fires. These are engaged in battle, and they know it—a battle that never ends. And while a warfare that goes on without truce necessarily develops its own jokes, informalities, callousnesses, disregard of wounds and gruesome sights, yet deep in their souls the units never forget that they are drilled and regimented for struggle. We stood the other evening with a Freeport man in the baggage com-

Consider the Commuter

partment at the front of a train leaving Brooklyn. We two had gained the bull's-eye window at the nose of the train and sombrely watched the sparkling panorama of lights along the track. Something had gone wrong with the schedule that evening, and the passengers of the 5:27 had been shunted to the 5:30. As fellow mariners will, we discussed famous breakdowns of old and the uncertainties of the commuter's life. "Yes," said our companion, "once you leave home you never know when you'll get back." And he smiled the passive, placable smile of the experienced commuter.

It is this reasonable and moderate temper that makes the commuter the seed wherewith a new generation shall be disseminated. He faces troubles manifold without embittered grumbling. His is a new kind of Puritanism, which endures hardship without dourness. When, on Christmas Eve, the train out of Jamaica was so packed that the aisle was one long mass of unwillingly embraced passengers, and even the car platforms were crowded with shivering wights, and the conductor buffeted his way as best he could over our toes and our parcels of tinsel balls, what was the general cry? Was it a yell against the railroad for not adding an extra brace of cars? No, it was good-natured banter of the perspiring little officer as he struggled to disentangle himself from forests of wedged legs. "You've got a fine, big family in here," they told him: "you ought to be proud of us." And there was a sorrowing Italian who had with him a string of seven children who had tunnelled and burrowed their way down the packed aisle of the smoking car and had got irretrievably scattered. The father was distracted. Here and there, down the length of the car, someone would discover an urchin and hold him up for inspection. "Is this one of them?" he would cry, and Italy would give assent. "Right!" And the children were agglomerated and piled in a heap in the middle of the car until such time as a thinning of the crowd permitted the anxious and blushing sire to reassemble them and reprove their truancy with Adriatic lightnings from his dark glowing eyes.

How pleasing is our commuter's simplicity! A cage of white mice, or a crated goat (such are to be seen now and then on the Jamaica platform) will engage his eye and give him keen amusement. Then there is that game always known (in the smoking car) as "pea-knuckle." The sight of four men playing will afford contemplative and apparently intense satisfaction to all near. They will lean diligently over seat-backs to watch every play of the cards. They will stand in the aisle to follow the game, with apparent comprehension. Then there are distinguished figures that move through the observant commuter's peep-show. There is the tall young man with the beaky nose, which (as Herrick said)

> Is the grace
> And proscenium of his face.

He is one of several light-hearted and carefree gentry who always sit together and are full of superb cheer. Those who travel sometimes with twinges of perplexity or skepticism are healed when they see the magnificent assurance of this creature. Every day we hear him

Consider the Commuter

making dates for his cronies to meet him at lunch time, and in the evening we see him towering above the throng at the gate. We like his confident air toward life, though he is still a little too jocular to be a typical commuter.

But the commuter, though simple and anxious to be pleased, is shrewdly alert. Every now and then they shuffle the trains at Jamaica just to keep him guessing and sharpen his faculty of judging whether this train goes to Brooklyn or Penn Station. His decisions have to be made rapidly. We are speaking now of Long Island commuters, whom we know best; but commuters are the same wherever you find them. The Jersey commuter has had his own celebrant in Joyce Kilmer, and we hope that he knows Joyce's pleasant essay on the subject which was published in that little book, "The Circus and Other Essays." But we gainsay the right of Staten Islanders to be classed as commuters. These are a proud and active sort who are really seafarers, not commuters. Fogs and ice floes make them blench a little; but the less romantic troubles of broken brake-shoes leave them unscotched.

Of Long Island commuters there are two classes: those who travel to Penn Station, those who travel to Brooklyn. Let it not be denied, there is a certain air of aristocracy about the Penn Station clique that we cannot waive. Their tastes are more delicate. The train-boy from Penn Station cries aloud "Choice, delicious apples," which seems to us almost an affectation compared to the hoarse yell of our Brooklyn news-agents imploring "Have a comic cartoon book, 'Mutt and Jeff,' 'Bringing Up Father,' choclut-covered cherries!'' The club cars all go to Penn Station: there would be a general apoplexy in the lowly terminal at Atlantic Avenue if one of those vehicles were seen there. People are often seen (on the Penn Station branch) who look exactly like the advertisements in *Vanity Fair*. Yet we, for our humility, have treasures of our own, such as the brightly lighted little shops along Atlantic Avenue and a station with the poetic name of Autumn Avenue. The Brooklyn commuter points with pride to his monthly ticket, which is distinguished from that of the Penn Station nobility by a red badge of courage— a bright red stripe. On the Penn Station branch they often punch the tickets with little diamond-shaped holes; but on our line the punch is in the form of a heart.

When the humble commuter who is accustomed to travelling via Brooklyn is diverted from his accustomed orbit, and goes by way of the Pennsylvania Station, what surprising excitements are his. The enormousness of the crowd at Penn Station around 5 P. M. causes him to realize that what he had thought, in his innocent Brooklyn fashion, was a considerable mob, was nothing more than a trifling scuffle. But he notes with pleasure the Penn Station habit of letting people through the gate before the train comes in, so that one may stand in comparative comfort and coolness downstairs on the train platform. Here a vision of luxury greets his eyes that could not possibly be imagined at the Brooklyn terminal—the Lehigh Valley dining car that stands on a neighbouring track, the pink candles lit on the tables, the shining water carafes, the white-coated stewards at attention. At the car's kitchen window lolls a young coloured boy in a chef's hat, surveying the files of proletarian commuters with a glorious calmness of scorn and superiority. His mood of sanguine assurance and self-esteem is so complete, so unruffled, and so composed that we cannot help loving him. Lucky youth, devoid of cares, responsibilities, and chagrins! Does he not belong to the conquering class that has us all under its thumb? What does it matter that he (probably) knows less about cooking than you or I? He gazes with glorious cheer upon the wretched middle class, and as our train rolls away we see him still gazing across the darkling cellars of the station with that untroubled gleam of condescension, his eyes seeming (as we look back at them) as large and white and unspeculative as billiard balls.

In the eye of one commuter, the 12:50 SATURDAY ONLY is the most exciting train of all. What a gay, heavily-bundled, and loquacious crowd it is that gathers by the gate at the Atlantic Avenue terminal. There is a holiday spirit among the throng, which pants a little after the battle down and up those steps leading from the subway. (What a fine sight, incidentally, is the stag-like stout man who always leaps from the train first and speeds scuddingly along the platform, to reach the stairs before any one else.) Here is the man who always carries a blue cardboard box full of chicks. Their plaintive chirpings sound shrill and disconsolate. There is such a piercing sorrow and perplexity in their persistent query that one knows they have the true souls of minor poets. Here are two cheerful stenographers off to Rockaway for the week-end. They are rather sarcastic about another young woman of their party who always insists on sleeping under sixteen blankets when at the shore.

But the high point of the trip comes when one changes at Jamaica, there boarding the 1:15 for Salamis. This is the train that on Saturdays takes back the two famous club cars, known to all travellers on the Oyster Bay route. Behind partly drawn blinds the luncheon tables are spread; one gets narrow glimpses of the great ones of the Island at their tiffin. This is a militant moment for the white-jacketed steward of the club car. On Saturdays there are always some strangers, unaccustomed to the ways of this train, who regard the two wagons of luxury as a personal affront. When they find all the seats in the other cars filled they sternly desire to storm the door of the club car, where the proud steward stands on guard. "What's the matter with this car?" they say. "Nothing's the matter with it," he replies. Other more humble commuters stand in the vestibule, enjoying these little arguments. It is always quite delightful to see the indignation of these gallant creatures, their faces seamed with irritation to think that there should be a holy of holies into which they may not tread.

A proud man, and a high-spirited, is the conductor of the 4:27 on weekdays. This train, after leaving Jamaica, does not stop until Salamis is reached. It attains such magnificent speed that it always gets to Salamis a couple of minutes ahead of time. Then

Consider the Commuter

stands the conductor on the platform, watch in hand,
receiving the plaudits of those who get off. The Sa-
lamites have to stand patiently beside the train—it is
a level crossing—until it moves on. This is the daily
glory of this conductor, as he stands, watch in one hand,
the other hand on the signal cord, waiting for Time to
catch up with him. "*Some* train," we cry up at him;
he tries not to look pleased, but he is a happy man.
Then he pulls the cord and glides away.

Among other articulations in the anatomy of commuting, we mention the fact that no good trainman
ever speaks of a train *going* or *stopping* anywhere. He
says, "This train *makes* Sea Cliff and Glen Cove; it
don't make Salamis." To be more purist still, one
should refer to the train as "he" (as a kind of extension
of the engineer's personality, we suppose). If you want
to speak with the tongue of a veteran, you will say, "He
makes Sea Cliff and Glen Cove."

The commuter has a chance to observe all manner
of types among his brethren. On our line we all know
by sight the two fanatical checker players, bent happily
over their homemade board all the way to town. At
Jamaica they are so absorbed in play that the conductor
—this is the conductor who is so nervous about missing a fare and asks everyone three times if his ticket
has been punched—has to rout them out to change to
the Brooklyn train. "How's the game this morning?"
says someone. "Oh, I was just trimming him, but
they made us change." However thick the throng,
these two always manage to find seats together. They
are still hard at it when Atlantic Avenue is reached,

[175]

furiously playing the last moves as the rest file out. Then there is the humorous news-agent who takes charge of the smoking car between Jamaica and Oyster Bay. There is some mysterious little game that he conducts with his clients. Very solemnly he passes down the aisle distributing rolled-up strips of paper among the card players. By and by it transpires that some one has won a box of candy. Just how this is done we know not. Speaking of card players, observe the gaze of anguish on the outpost. He dashes ahead, grabs two facing seats and sits in one with a face contorted with anxiety for fear that the others will be too late to join him. As soon as a card game is started there are always a half dozen other men who watch it, following every play with painful scrutiny. It seems that watching other people play cards is the most absorbing amusement known to the commuter.

Then there is the man who carries a heavy bag packed with books. A queer creature, this. Day by day he lugs that bag with him yet spends all his time reading the papers and rarely using the books he carries. His pipe always goes out just as he reaches his station; frantically he tries to fill and light it before the train stops. Sometimes he digs deeply into the bag and brings out a large slab of chocolate, which he eats with an air of being slightly ashamed of himself. The oddities of this person do not amuse us any the less because he happens to be ourself.

So fares the commuter: a figure as international as the teddy bear. He has his own consolations—of a morning when he climbs briskly upward from his dark tunnel and sees the sunlight upon the spread wings of the Telephone and Telegraph Building's statue, and moves again into the stirring pearl and blue of New York's lucid air. And at night, though drooping a little in the heat and dimness of those Oyster Bay smoking cars, he is dumped down and set free. As he climbs the long hill and tunes his thoughts in order, the sky is a froth of stars.

THE PERMANENCE OF POETRY

WE HEARD a critic remark that no great sonnets are being written nowadays. What (he said morosely) is there in the way of a recent sonnet that is worthy to take its place in the anthologies of the future beside those of Sir Philip Sidney, Milton, Wordsworth, Keats, Mrs. Browning, Louise Guiney, Rupert Brooke, or Lizette Reese? (These were the names he mentioned.)

This moves us to ask, how can you tell? It takes time for any poem to grow and ripen and find its place in the language. It will be for those of a hundred or more years hence to say what are the great poems of our present day. If a sonnet has the true vitality in it, it will gather association and richness about it as it traces

[178]

The Permanence of Poetry

its slender golden path through the minds of readers. It settles itself comfortably into the literary landscape, incorporates itself subtly into the unconscious thought of men, becomes corpuscular in the blood of the language. It comes down to us in the accent of those who have loved and quoted it, invigorated by our subtle sense of the permanent rightness of its phrasing and our knowledge of the pleasure it has given to thousands of others. The more it is quoted, the better it seems.

All this is a slow process and an inscrutable. No one has ever given us a continuous history of any particular poem, tracing its history and adventures after its first publication—the places it has been quoted, the hearts it has rejoiced. It could only be done by an infinity of toil and a prodigal largesse to clipping bureaus. It would be a fascinating study, showing how some poems have fought for their lives against the evaporation of Time, and how they have come through, sometimes, because they were carried and cherished in one or two appreciative hearts. But the point to bear in mind is, the whole question of the permanence of poetry is largely in the hands of chance. If you are interested to observe the case of some really first-class poetry which has been struggling for recognition and yet shows, so far, no sign of breaking through into the clear light of lasting love and remembrance, look at the poems of James Elroy Flecker.

Generally speaking, one law is plain: that it is not until the poet himself and all who knew him are dead, and his lines speak only with the naked and impersonal appeal of ink, that his value to the race as a permanent pleasure can be justly appraised.

There is one more point that perhaps is worth making. It is significant of human experience that the race instinctively demands, in most of the poetry that it cares to take along with it as permanent baggage, a certain honourable sobriety of mood. Consider Mr. Burton E. Stevenson's great "Home Book of Verse," that magnificent anthology which may be taken as fairly indicative of general taste in these matters. In nearly 4,000 pages of poetry only three or four hundred are cynical or satirical in temper. Humanity as a whole likes to make the best of a bad job: it grins somewhat ruefully at the bitter and the sardonic; but when it is packing its trunk for the next generation it finds most room for those poets who have somehow contrived to find beauty and not mockery in the inner sanctities of human life and passion. This thought comes to us on reading Aldous Huxley's brilliant and hugely entertaining book of poems called "Leda." There is no more brilliant young poet writing to-day; his title poem is nothing less than extraordinary in pagan and pictorial beauty, but as a whole the cynical and scoffish tone of carnal drollery which gives the book its appeal to the humorously inclined makes a very dubious sandal for a poet planning a long-distance run. Please note that we are not taking sides in any argument: we ourself admire Mr. Huxley's poems enormously; but we are simply trying, clumsily, to state what seem to us some of the conditions attaching to the permanence of beauty as arranged in words.

The Permanence of Poetry

It is not to be supposed that you have done your possible when you have read a great poem once—or ten times. A great poem is like a briar pipe—it darkens and mellows and sweetens with use. You fill it with your own glowing associations and glosses, and the strong juices seep through, staining and gilding the grain and fibre of the words.

BOOKS OF THE SEA

THE National Marine League asks, What are the ten best books of the sea? Without pondering very deeply on the matter, and confining ourself to prose, we would suggest the following as our own favourites:

Typhoon, by Joseph Conrad
The Nigger of the "Narcissus," by Joseph Conrad
The Mirror of the Sea, by Joseph Conrad
Captains Courageous, by Rudyard Kipling
The Brassbounder, by David W. Bone

[182]

Books of the Sea

Salt of the Sea, by Morley Roberts
Mr. Midshipman Easy, by Captain Marryat
The Wreck of the "Grosvenor," by Clark Russell
Moby Dick, by Herman Melville
An Ocean Tramp, by William McFee.

If one is allowed to include books that deal partially with salt water, one would have to add "Treasure Island," "Casuals of the Sea," by McFee, and "Old Junk," by Tomlinson. The kind of shallow-water sea tales that we love to read after supper, with our feet on the nearest chair and a decent supply of tobacco handy, are the delicious stories by W. W. Jacobs. Dana's "Two Years Before the Mast," which is spoken of as a classic, we have never read. We have always had a suspicion of it, we don't know why. Before we tackle it we shall re-read "The Water Babies." We have always found a good deal of innocent cheer in the passages in John Woolman's Journal describing his voyage from Philadelphia to London in 1772. Friend Woolman, like the sturdy Quaker that he was, was horrified (when he went to have a look at the ship *Mary and Elizabeth*) to find "sundry sorts of carved work and imagery" on that part of the vessel where the cabins were; and in the cabins themselves he observed "some superfluity of workmanship of several sorts." This subjected his mind to "a deep exercise," and he decided that he would have to take passage in the steerage instead of the cabin. Having ourself made use of the steerage aforetime, both in the *Mauretania* and humbler vessels, we feel a certain kindred sympathy for his experiences. We have always enjoyed his remark: "The wind now blew vehemently, and the sea wrought to that degree that an awful seriousness prevailed."

To come to poetry, we suppose that the greatest sea-poet who never ventured on anything more perilous than a ferry-boat was Walt Whitman. Walt, one likes to think, would have been horribly sea-sick if he had ventured out beyond the harbour buoy. A good deal of Walt's tempestuous uproar about the glories of America was undoubtedly due to the fact that he had never seen anything else. Speaking of Walt reminds us that one book of the sea that we have never read (for the best of reasons: it has not been written) might be done by Thomas Mosher, the veteran tippler of literary minims. Mr. Mosher, we understand, "followed" the sea in his youth. Not long ago, when Mr. Mosher published that exquisite facsimile of the 1855 "Leaves of Grass," we asked him when and how he first came in contact with Whitman's work. He said:

I don't suppose there was anything particularly interesting about my first acquaintance with Whitman, which at 14 years of age I made in my old family mansion situated at Smith's Corner, America. I had been taking "The Galaxy" from its start, only a few months previous to the date I mention. I can still see myself in the sitting room of the old house. Smith's Cor., America, I will remind you, is a portion of Biddeford, Me. An extra "d" has got into the old English name—which, by the way, only a year later I passed through after a shipwreck on the Devonshire coast. (That was in 1867.) No one ever told me anything about Walt.

Books of the Sea

These amateurish speculations on maritime books are of no value except for the fact that they elicited an interesting letter from an expert on these matters. William McFee wrote us as follows:—

"The first thing I laid my hands on this evening, while hunting for some forgotten nugget of wisdom in my note-books filled with Mediterranean brine, was that list of books for a projected sea library. Perpend. . . .

The Sea Farer's Library

Tom Cringle's Log . . . . Michael Scott
Two Years Before the Mast . . . . Dana
Midshipman Easy . . . . Marryat
Captains Courageous . . . . Kipling
The Flying Cloud . . . . Morley Roberts
The Cruise of the Cachalot . . . . Frank T. Bullen
Log of a Sea Waif . . . . Frank T. Bullen
The Salving of a Derelict . . . . Maurice Drake
The Grain Carriers . . . . Edward Noble
Marooned . . . . Clark Russell
Typhoon . . . . Conrad
Toilers of the Sea . . . . Hugo
An Iceland Fisherman . . . . Loti
The Sea Surgeon . . . . D'Annunzio
The Sea Hawk . . . . Sabatini

"A good many of these need no comment. Attention is drawn not to the individual items, but to the balance of the whole. That is the test of a list. But there is a good balance, a balance of power, and a balance of mere weight or prestige. It is the power we are after here. Regard for a moment the way 'Tom Cringle' balances Dana's laconic record of facts. No power on earth could hold 'Tom Cringle' to facts, with the result that his story is more truly a representation of sea life in the old navy than a ton of statistics. He has the seaman's mind, which Dana had not.

"Then again 'Captains Courageous' and 'The Flying Cloud' balance each other with temperamental exactitude. Each is a fine account of sea-doings with a touch of fiction to keep the sailor reading, neither of them in the very highest class. 'The Cruise of the Cachalot' is balanced by the 'Log of a Sea Waif,' each in Bullen's happier and less evangelical vein. I was obliged to exclude 'With Christ at Sea,' not because it is religious, but because it does not balance. It would give the whole list a most pronounced 'list,' if you will pardon the unpardonable. . . . I regret this because 'With Christ at Sea' has some things in it which transcend anything else Bullen ever wrote.

"Now we come to a couple of books possibly requiring a little explanation. 'The Salving of a Derelict' is a remarkably able story of a man's reclamation. I believe Maurice Drake won a publisher's prize with it as a first novel some years ago. It was a winner among the apprentices, I remember. 'The Grain Carriers' is a grim story of greedy owners and an unseaworthy ship by an ex-master mariner whose 'Chains,' while not a sea story, is tinged with the glamour of South American shipping, and is obviously a work written under the influence of Joseph Conrad. 'Marooned' and 'Typhoon' balance (only you mustn't be too critical) as examples of the old and new methods of telling a sea story.

"'The Sea Surgeon' is one of a collection of stories about the Pescarese, which D'Annunzio wrote years ago. They are utterly unlike 'Il Fuoco' and the other absurd tales on which translators waste their time. In passing one is permitted to complain of the persistent ill-fortune Italian novelists suffer at the hands of their English translators.

Books of the Sea

"Assuming, however, that our seafarer wants a book or two of what is euphemistically termed 'non-fiction,' here are a few which will do him no harm:

"Southey's 'Life of Nelson.'

"'The Influence of Sea Power Upon History,'Mahan.

"Admiral Lord Beresford's 'Memoirs.'

"The Diary of Samuel Pepys, F. R. S., Secretary to the Admiralty in the Reign of Charles II and James II. It is most grievously overlooked that Samuel was the first to draft a naval Rate Book, which is a sort of indexed lexicon of everything one needs 'for fighting and sea-going efficiency.' And it is a pleasure, chastened by occasional fits of ill-temper, to discover that the present British Naval Rate Book hath in it divers synonyms coeval with Samuel and his merry monarchs. As when the present writer tried to order some hammer-handles and discovered after much tribulation that the correct naval equivalent for such is 'ash-helms.' Whereupon he toilfully rewrote his requisitions 'and so to bed.'

"Another suggestion I might make is a volume to be compiled, containing the following chapters:

    I. "Landsmen Admirals," Generals Blake and Monk.

    II. "A Dutch Triumvirate," Van Tromp, De Witt and De Ruyter.

    III. "Napoleon as a Sea Tactician."

    IV. "Decatur and the Mediterranean Pirates."

    V. "The Chesapeake and the Shannon."

    VI. "The Spanish-American Naval Actions."

    VII. "The Russo-Japanese Naval Actions."

    VIII. "The Turko-Italian Naval Actions."

Conclusion. "Short Biography of Josephus Daniels."

"Only deep-water sailors would be able to take this suggested library to sea with them, because a sailor only reads at sea. When the landward breeze brings the odours of alien lands through the open scuttle one closes the book, and if one is a normal and rational kind of chap and the quarantine regulations permit, goes ashore."

Gruesome as anything in any seafaring pirate yarn is Trelawny's description (in "Recollections of the Last Days of Shelley and Byron") of the burning of Shelley's body on the seashore near Via Reggio. The other day, in company with two like-minded innocents, we visited a bookshop on John Street where we found three battered copies of this great book, and each bought one, with shouts of joy. The following day, still having the book with us, we dropped in to see the learned and hospitable Dr. Rosenbach at his new and magnificent thesaurus at 273 Madison Avenue. We showed him the book, because every time one shows the doctor a book he can startle you by countering with its original manuscript or something of that sort. We said something about Shelley and Trelawny, in the hope of starting him off. He smiled gently and drew out a volume from a shelf. It was the copy of "Prometheus Unbound" that Shelley had given Trelawny in July, 1822, with an inscription. As the poet was drowned on July 8, 1822, it probably was the last book he ever gave away.

One wonders what may have become of the log of the American clipper that Shelley and Trelawny visited in the harbour of Leghorn shortly before Shelley's death. Shelley had said something in praise of George Washington, to which the sturdy Yankee skipper replied: "Stranger, truer words were never spoken; there is dry rot in all the main timbers of the Old World, and none of you will do any good till you are docked, refitted, and annexed to the New. You must log that song you sang; there ain't many Britishers that will say as much of the man that whipped them; so just set these lines down in the log!"

Whereupon Shelley autographed the skipper's log for him, with some sentiments presumably gratifying to American pride, and drank some "cool peach brandy." It was his last drink.

We ourself, just as much as Shelley, enjoy visiting ships, and have had some surprising adventures in so doing. We remember very clearly our first call upon William McFee, when he was First Assistant Engineer in S. S. *Turrialba*. But getting aboard vessels is a much more complicated and diplomatic task than it was in Shelley's day. Even when armed with Mr. McFee's autographed card, it was by no means easy. We went dutifully up to the office of the United Fruit Company at Pier 9, to apply for a pass, and were surveyed with grim suspicion. Why, we asked gently, in these peaceful times is it so difficult to visit a friend who happens to be in a ship? Prohibition, said the candid clerk, and a whole province of human guile was thereby made plain to our shrinking mind. Mortals incline readily to sin, it seems, and apparently evil and base men will even go so far as to pretend a friendship with those who go down to wet territory in ships, simply for the sake of —well, we cannot bring ourself to mention it. "How do you know Mr. McFee wants to see you?" we were asked. Luckily we had Mac's card to prove it.

Plum Pudding

We had long wanted to see Mr. McFee in his sea-going quarters, where he writes his books and essays (so finely flavoured with a rich ironical skepticism as to the virtues of folk who live on shore). Never was a literary sanctum less like the pretentious studios of the imitation litterateurs. In a small cabin stood our friend, in his working dungarees (if that is what they are called) talking briskly with the Chief and another engineer. The conversation, in which we were immediately engulfed, was so vivacious that we had small chance to examine the surroundings as we would have liked to. But save for the typewriter on the desk and a few books in a rack, there was nothing to suggest literature. "Plutarch's Lives," we noticed—a favourite of Mac's since boyhood; Frank Harris's "The Bomb" (which, however, the Chief insisted belonged to him), E. S. Martin's "Windfalls of Observation," and some engineering works. We envied Mac the little reading lamp at the head of his bunk.

We wish some of the soft-handed literary people who bleat about only being able to write in carefully purged and decorated surroundings could have a look at that stateroom. In just such compartments Mr. McFee has written for years, and expected to finish that night (in the two hours each day that he is able to devote to writing) his tale, "Captain Macedoine's Daughter." As we talked there was a constant procession of in-comers, most of them seeming to the opaque observation of the layman to be firemen discussing matters of overtime. On the desk lay an amusing memorandum, which the Chief referred to jocularly as one

Books of the Sea

of Mac's "works," anent some problem of whether the donkeyman was due certain overtime on a Sunday when the *Turrialba* lay in Hampton Roads waiting for coal. On the cabin door was a carefully typed list marked in Mr. McFee's hand "Work to Do." It began something like this:

Main Engine Pump Link Brasses
Fill Up Main Engine Feed Pump and Bilge Rams
Open and Scale After Port Boiler
Main Circulator Impeller to Examine
Hydrokineter Valve on Centre Boiler to be Rejointed

The delightful thing about Mr. McFee is that he can turn from these things, which he knows and loves, to talk about literary problems, and can out-talk most literary critics at their own game.

He took us through his shining engines, showing us some of the beauty spots—the Weir pumps and the refrigerating machinery and the thrust-blocks (we hope we have these right), unconsciously inflicting upon us something of the pain it gives the bungling jack of several trades when he sees a man who is so fine a master not merely of one, but of two—two seemingly diverse, but in which the spirit of faith and service are the same. "She's a bonny ship," he said, and his face was lit with sincerity as he said it. Then he washed his hands and changed into shore clothes and we went up to Frank's, where we had pork and beans and talked about Sir Thomas Browne.

FALLACIOUS MEDITATIONS ON CRITICISM

I

THERE are never, at any time and place, more than a few literary critics of genuine incision, taste, and instinct; and these qualities, rare enough in themselves, are further debilitated, in many cases, by excessive geniality or indigestion. The ideal literary critic should be guarded as carefully as a delicate thermal instrument at the Weather Bureau; his meals, friendships, underwear, and bank account should all be supervised by experts and advisedly maintained at a temperate mean. In the Almost Perfect State (so many phases of which have been deliciously delineated by Mr. Marquis) a critic seen to become over-exhilarated at the dining table or to address any author by his first name would promptly be haled from the room by a commissionaire lest his intellectual acuity become blunted by emotion.

The unfortunate habit of critics being also human beings has done a great deal to impair their value to the public. For other human beings we all nourish a secret disrespect. And therefore it is well that the world should be reminded now and then of the dignity and purity of the critic's function. The critic's duty is not merely to tabulate literary material according to some convenient scale of proved niceties; but to discern the ratio existing in any given work between possibility and performance; between the standard the author might justly have been expected to achieve and the standard he actually attained. There are hierarchies and lower archies. A pint pot, full (it is no new observation), is just as full as a bathtub full. And the first duty of the critic is to determine and make plain to the reader the frame of mind in which the author approached his task.

Just as a ray of sunshine across a room reveals, in air that seemed clear, innumerable motes of golden dancing dust and filament, so the bright beam of a great critic shows us the unsuspected floating atoms of temperament in the mind of a great writer. The popular understanding of the word *criticize* is to find fault, to pettifog. As usual, the popular mind is only partly right. The true critic is the tender curator and warden of all that is worthy in letters. His function is sacramental, like the sweeping of a hearth. He keeps the hearth clean and nourishes the fire. It is a holy fire, for its fuel is men's hearts.

Plum Pudding

It seems to us probable that under present conditions the cause of literature is more likely to suffer from injudicious and excessive praise rather than from churlish and savage criticism. It seems to us (and we say this with certain misgivings as to enthusiasms of our own) that there are many reviewers whose honest zeal for the discovering of masterpieces is so keen that they are likely to burst into superlatives half a dozen times a year and hail as a flaming genius some perfectly worthy creature, who might, if he were given a little stiff discipline, develop into a writer of best-readers rather than best-sellers. Too resounding praise is often more damning than faint praise. The writer who has any honest intentions is more likely to be helped by a little judicious acid now and then than by cartloads of honey. Let us be candid and personal. When someone in *The New Republic* spoke of some essays of our own as "blowzy" we were moved for a few moments to an honest self-scrutiny and repentance. Were we really blowzy, we said to ourself? We did not know exactly what this meant, and there was no dictionary handy. But the word gave us a picture of a fat, ruddy beggar-wench trudging through wind and rain, probably on the way to a tavern; and we determined, with modest sincerity, to be less like that in future.

The good old profession of criticism tends, in the hands of the younger generation, toward too fulsome ejaculations of hurrahs and hyperboles. It is a fine thing, of course, that new talent should so swiftly win its recognition; yet we think we are not wholly wrong in believing that many a delicate and promising writer has been hurried into third-rate work, into women's magazine serials and cheap sordid sensationalism, by a hasty overcapitalization of the reviewer's shouts. For our own part, we do not feel any too sure of our ability to recognize really great work when we first see it. We have often wondered, if we had been journalizing in 1855 when "Leaves of Grass" appeared, would we have been able to see what it meant, or wouldn't we have been more likely to fill our column with japeries at the expense of Walt's obvious absurdities, missing all the finer grain? It took a man like Emerson to see what Walt was up to.

There were many who didn't. Henry James, for instance, wrote a review of "Drum Taps" in the *Nation*, November 16, 1865. In the lusty heyday and assurance of twenty-two years, he laid the birch on smartly. It is just a little saddening to find that even so clearsighted an observer as Henry James could not see through the chaotic form of Whitman to the great vision and throbbing music that seem so plain to us to-day. Whitman himself, writing about "Drum Taps" before its publication, said, "Its passion has the indispensable merit that though to the ordinary reader let loose with wildest abandon, the true artist can see that it is yet under control." With this, evidently, the young Henry James did not agree. He wrote:

It has been a melancholy task to read this book; and it is a still more melancholy one to write about it. Perhaps since the day of Mr. Tupper's "Philosophy" there has been no more difficult reading of the poetic sort. It exhibits the effort of an essentially prosaic mind to lift itself, by a prolonged muscular strain, into poetry. Like hundreds of other good patriots, Mr. Walt Whitman has imagined that a certain amount of violent sympathy with the great deeds and sufferings of our soldiers, and of admiration for our national energy, together with a ready command of picturesque language, are sufficient inspiration for a poet. . . . But he is not a poet who merely reiterates these plain facts *ore rotundo*. He only sings them worthily who views them from a height. . . . Mr. Whitman is very fond of blowing his own trumpet, and he has made very explicit claims for his book. . . . . The frequent capitals are the only marks of verse in Mr. Whitman's writing. There is, fortunately, but one attempt at rhyme. . . . Each line starts off by itself, in resolute independence of its companions, without a visible goal . . . it begins like verse and turns out to be arrant prose. It is more like Mr. Tupper's proverbs than anything we have met. . . . No triumph, however small, is won but through the exercise of art, and this volume is an offence against art. . . . We look in vain through the book for a single idea. We find nothing but flashy imitations of ideas. We find a medley of extravagances and commonplaces.

We do not know whether H. J. ever recanted this very youthful disposal of old Walt. The only importance of it at this moment seems to us this: that appreciation of all kinds of art is so tenderly interwoven with inherited respect for the traditional forms of expression by which they are conveyed that a new and surprising vehicle quite unfits most observers for any reasonable assessment of the passenger.

As for Walt himself, he was quite unabashed by this or any other onslaught. He was not gleg at argument,

Fallacious Meditations on Criticism

and probably rolled up the issue of the *Nation* in his pocket and went down to Coney Island to lie on the sand and muse (but no, we forget, it was November!). In the same issue of the *Nation* he doubtless read, in the "Literary Notes," that "Poems Relating to the American Revolution," by Philip Freneau, was "in press under the scholarly editing of Evart A. Duyckinck to form a complete presentment of the genius of an author whose influence in the affairs of his time would alone impart a lasting value to his works." At this Walt smiled gently to himself, wondered how soon " When Lilacs Last in the Dooryard Bloomed" would get into the anthologies, and "sped to the certainties suitable to him."

II

These miscellaneous thoughts on the fallibility of critics were suggested to us by finding some old bound volumes of the *Edinburgh Review* on a bookstall, five cents each. In the issue for November, 1814, we read with relish what the *Review* had to say about Wordsworth's "Excursion." These are a few excerpts:

This will never do. . . . The case of Mr. Wordsworth, we perceive, is now manifestly hopeless; and we give him up as altogether incurable, and beyond the power of criticism . . . making up our minds, though with the most sincere pain and reluctance, to consider him as finally lost to the good cause of poetry. . . . The volume before us, if we were to describe it very shortly, we should characterize as a tissue of moral and devotional ravings, in which innumerable changes are rung upon a few very simple and familiar ideas.

Plum Pudding

The world of readers has not ratified Jeffrey's savage comments on "The Excursion," for (to reckon only by the purse) any frequenter of old bookshops can pick up that original issue of the *Edinburgh Review* for a few cents, while the other day we saw a first edition of the maligned "Excursion" sold for thirty dollars. A hundred years ago it was the critic's pleasure to drub authors with cruel and unnecessary vigour. But we think that almost equal harm can be done by the modern method of hailing a new "genius" every three weeks.

For example, there is something subtly troublesome to us in the remark that Sinclair Lewis made about Evelyn Scott's novel, "The Narrow House." The publishers have used it as an advertising slogan, and the words have somehow buzzed their way into our head:

"Salute to Evelyn Scott: she belongs, she understands, she is definitely an artist."

We have been going about our daily affairs, climbing subway stairs, dodging motor trucks, ordering platters of stewed rhubarb, with that refrain recurring and recurring. *Salute to Evelyn Scott!* (we say to ourself as we stand in line at the bank, waiting to cash a small check). *She belongs, she understands.* And then, as we go away, pensively counting the money (they've got some clean Ones down at our bank, by the way; we don't know whether the larger denominations are clean or not, we haven't seen any since Christmas), we find ourself mumbling, *She is definitely an artist.*

We wonder why that pronouncement annoys us so.

Fallacious Meditations on Criticism

We haven't read all Mrs. Scott's book yet, and doubt our strength to do so. It is a riot of morbid surgery by a fumbling scalpel: great powers of observation are put to grotesque misuse. It is crammed with faithful particulars neither relevant nor interesting. (Who sees so little as he who looks through a microscope?) At first we thought, hopefully, that it was a bit of excellent spoof; then, regretfully, we began to realize that not only the publishers but even the author take it seriously. It feels as though it had been written by one of the new school of Chicago realists. It is disheartening that so influential a person as Mr. Lewis should be fooled by this sort of thing.

So there is something intensely irritating to us (although we admire Mr. Lewis) in that "*She belongs, she understands, she is definitely an artist.*" In the first place, that use of the word *artist* as referring to a writer always gives us qualms unless used with great care. Then again, *She belongs* somehow seems to intimate that there is a registered clique of authors, preferably those who come down pretty heavily upon the disagreeable facts of life and catalogue them with gluttonous care, which group is the only one that counts. Now we are strong for disagreeable facts. We know a great many. But somehow we cannot shake ourself loose from the instinctive conviction that imagination is the without-which-nothing of the art of fiction. Miss Stella Benson is one who is not unobservant of disagreeables, but when she writes she can convey her satire in flashing, fantastic absurdity, in a heavenly chiding so delicate and subtle that the victim hardly knows he is being chidden. The photographic facsimile of life always seems to us the lesser art, because it is so plainly the easier course.

We fear we are not acute enough to explain just why it is that Mr. Lewis's salute to Mrs. Scott bothers us so. But it does bother us a good deal. We have nourished ourself, in the main, upon the work of two modern writers: Robert Louis Stevenson and Joseph Conrad; we like to apply as a test such theories as we have been able to glean from those writers. Faulty and erring as we are, we always rise from Mr. Conrad's books purged and, for the moment, strengthened. Apparent in him are that manly and honourable virtue, that strict saline truth and scrupulous regard for life, that liberation from cant, which seem to be inbred in those who have suffered the exacting discipline of the hostile sea. Certainly Conrad cannot be called a writer who has neglected the tragic side of things. Yet in his "Notes on Life and Letters," we find this:

What one feels so hopelessly barren in declared pessimism is just its arrogance. It seems as if the discovery made by many men at various times that there is much evil in the world were a source of proud and unholy joy unto some of the modern writers. That frame of mind is not the proper one in which to approach seriously the art of fiction. . . . To be hopeful in an artistic sense it is not necessary to think that the world is good. It is enough to believe that there is no impossibility of its being made so. . . . I would ask that in his dealings with mankind he [the writer] should be capable of giving a tender recognition to their obscure virtues. I would not have him impatient with their small failings and scornful of their errors.

We fear that our mild protest is rather mixed and muddled. But what we darkly feel is this: that no author "belongs," or "understands," or is "definitely an artist" who merely makes the phantoms of his imagination paltry or ridiculous. They may be paltry, but they must also be pitiable; they may be ridiculous, but they must also be tragic. Many authors have fallen from the sublime to the ridiculous; but, as Mr. Chesterton magnificently said, in order to make that descent they must first reach the sublime.

LETTING OUT THE FURNACE

THE prudent commuter (and all commuters **are** prudent, for the others are soon weeded out by the rigours of that way of life) keeps the furnace going until early May in these latitudes—assuming that there are small children in the house. None of those April hot waves can fool him; he knows that, with cunning management, two or three shovelfuls of coal a day will nurse the fire along, and there it is in case of a sudden chilly squall. But when at last he lets the fire die, and after its six months of constant and honourable service the old boiler grows cold, the kindly glow fades and sinks downward out of sight under a crust of gray clinkers, our friend muses tenderly in his cellar, sitting on a packing case.

Letting Out the Furnace

He thinks, first, how odd it is that when he said to himself, "We might as well let the fire go out," it kept on sturdily burning, without attention or fuel, for a day and a half; whereas if he had, earlier in the season, neglected it even for a few hours, all would have been cold and silent. He remembers, for instance, the tragic evening with the mercury around zero, when, having (after supper) arranged everything at full blast and all radiators comfortably sizzling, he lay down on his couch to read Leonard Merrick, intending to give all hands a warm house for the night. Very well; but when he woke up around 2 A. M. and heard the tenor winds singing through the woodland, how anxiously he stumbled down the cellar stairs, fearing the worst. His fears were justified. There, on top of the thick bed of silvery ashes, lay the last pallid rose of fire. For as every pyrophil has noted, when the draught is left on, the fire flees upward, leaving its final glow at the top; but when all draughts are shut off, it sinkst downward, shyly hiding in the heart of the mass.

So he stood, still drowsily aghast, while Gissing (the synthetic dog) frolicked merrily about his unresponsive shins, deeming this just one more of those surprising entertainments arranged for his delight.

Now, on such an occasion the experienced commuter makes the best of a bad job, knowing there is little to be gained by trying to cherish and succour a feeble remnant of fire. He will manfully jettison the whole business, filling the cellar with the crash of shunting ashes and the clatter of splitting kindling. But this pitiable creature still thought that mayhap he could, by sedulous care and coaxing, revive the dying spark. With such black arts as were available he wrestled with the despondent glim. During this period of guilty and furtive strife he went quietly upstairs, and a voice spoke up from slumber. "Isn't the house very cold?" it said.

"Is it?" said this wretched creature, with great simulation of surprise. "Seems very comfortable to me."

"Well, I think you'd better send up some more heat," said this voice, in the tone of one accustomed to command.

"Right away," said the panic-stricken combustion engineer, and returned to his cellar, wondering whether he was suspected. How is it, he wondered, that ladies know instinctively, even when vested in several layers of blankets, if anything is wrong with the furnace? Another of the mysteries, said he, grimly, to the synthetic dog. By this time he knew full well (it was 3 A. M.) that there was naught for it but to decant the grateful of cinders and set to work on a new fire.

Such memories throng in the mind of the commuter as he surveys the dark form of his furnace, standing cold and dusty in the warm spring weather, and he cleans and drains it for the summer vacation. He remembers the lusty shout of winter winds, the clean and silver nakedness of January weather, the shining glow of the golden coals, the comfortable rustling and chuckle of the boiler when alive with a strong urgency of steam, the soft thud and click of the pipes when the pressure was rising before breakfast. And he meditates that these matters, though often the cause of grumbles at the time, were a part of that satisfying reality that makes life in the outposts a more honest thing than the artificial convenience of great apartment houses. The commuter, no less than the seaman, has fidelities of his own; and faithful, strict obedience to hard necessary formulæ favours the combined humility and self-respect that makes human virtue. The commuter is often a figure both tragic and absurd; but he has a rubric and discipline of his own. And when you see him grotesquely hasting for the 5:27 train, his inner impulse may be no less honourable than that of the ship's officer ascending the bridge for his watch under a dark speckle of open sky.

BY THE FIREPLACE

WE WERE contemplating our fireplace, in which some of the hearth-bricks are rather irregularly disposed; and we said to ourself, perhaps the bricklayer who built this noble fireplace worked like Ben Jonson, with a trowel in one hand and a copy of Horace in the other. That suggested to us that we had not read any Ben Jonson for a very long time: so we turned to "Every Man in His Humour" and "The Alchemist." Part of Jonson's notice "To the Reader" preceding "The Alchemist" struck us as equally valid as regards poetry to-day:

Thou wert never more fair in the way to be cozened, than in this age, in poetry; wherein . . . antics to run away from nature, and be afraid of her, is the only

point of art that tickles the spectators . . . For
they commend writers, as they do fencers or wrestlers;
who if they come in robustuously, and put for it with
a great deal of violence, are received for the braver fellows. . . . I deny not, but that these men, who
always seek to do more than enough, may some time
happen on some thing that is good, and great; but very
seldom . . . I give thee this warning, that there is
a great difference between those, that utter all they can,
however unfitly; and those that use election and a mean.
For it is only the disease of the unskilful, to think rude
things greater than polished; or scattered more numerous than composed.

Ben Jonson's perpetual allusions to tobacco always remind one of the odd circumstance that of
two such cronies as he and Will Shakespeare, one
should have mentioned tobacco continually, the
other not at all. Undoubtedly Ben smoked a particularly foul old pipe and was forever talking about
it, spouting his rank strangling "Cuban ebolition"
across the table; and Will, probably rather nice
in his personal habits, grew disgusted with the
habit.

At any rate, Shakespeare's silence on the subject has
always been a grief to smokers. At a time when we
were interested in that famous and innocent way of
wasting time, trying to discover ciphers in Shakespeare's
sonnets, we spent long cryptogrammarian evenings
seeking to prove some anagram or rebus by which the
Bard could be supposed to have concealed a mention
of tobacco. But the only lurking secret we ever discovered seemed to suggest that the sonnets had been

Plum Pudding

written by an ex-President of the United States. Observe the 131st sonnet:

Thou art as tyrannous, so as thou art
As those whose beauties proudly make them cruel;
For well thou know'st to my dear doting heart
Thou art the fairest and most precious jewel.

And evidently Shakespeare intended to begin the 51st sonnet with the same acrostic; but, with Elizabethan laxity, misspelled Mr. Taft's name as TOFT.

Reading Elizabethan literature always encourages one to proceed, even though decorously, with the use of the pun. Such screams of mirth as (we doubt not) greeted one of Ben Jonson's simpletons when he spoke of Roger Bacon as Rasher Bacon (we can hear them laughing, can't you?) are highly fortifying.

But we began by quoting Ben Jonson on poetry. The passage sent us to the bookcase to look up the "axioms" about poetry stated by another who was also, in spirit at least, an habitué of The Mermaid. In that famous letter from Keats to his publisher and friend John Taylor, February 27, 1818, there is a fine fluent outburst on the subject. All Keats lovers know these "axioms" already, but they cannot be quoted too often; and we copy them down with additional pleasure because not long ago, by the kindness of the two librarians who watch over one of the most marvellous private collections in the world—Mr. J. P. Morgan's—we saw the original letter itself:—

By the Fireplace

1st. I think poetry should surprise by a fine excess, and not by singularity. It should strike the reader as a wording of his own highest thoughts, and appear almost a remembrance.

2d. Its touches of beauty should never be half-way, thereby making the reader breathless, instead of content. The rise, the progress, the setting of Imagery should, like the sun, come natural to him, shine over him, and set soberly, although in magnificence, leaving him in the luxury of twilight. But it is easier to think what poetry should be than to write it—and this leads me to

Another axiom—That if poetry comes not as naturally as the leaves to a tree, it had better not come at all.

Some people can always find things to complain about. We have seen protests because the house in Rome where Keats died is used as a steamship office. We think it is rather appropriate. No man's mind ever set sail upon wider oceans of imagination. To paraphrase Emily Dickinson:

> Night after night his purple traffic
> Strews the landing with opal bales;
> Merchantmen poise upon horizons,
> Dip, and vanish with fairy sails.

Another pleasing fact is that while he was a medical student Keats lived in Bird-in-Hand Court, Cheapside —best known nowadays as the home of Simpson's, that magnificent chophouse. Who else, in modern times, came so close to holding unruffled in his hand the shy wild bird of Poetry?

A CITY NOTE-BOOK

WELL, now let us see in what respect we are richer to-day than we were yesterday.

Coming down Fifth Avenue on top of a bus, we saw a man absorbed in a book. Ha, we thought, here is our chance to see how bus reading compares to subway reading! After some manœuvering, we managed to get the seat behind the victim. The volume was "Every Man a King," by Orison Swett Marden, and the uncrowned monarch reading it was busy with the thirteenth chapter, to wit: "Thoughts Radiate as Influence." We did a little radiating of our own, and it seemed to reach him, for presently he grew uneasy, put the volume carefully away in a brief-case, and (as far as we could see) struck out toward his kingdom, which apparently lay on the north shore of Forty-second Street.

We felt then that we would recuperate by glancing at

A City Note-book

a little literature. So we made our way toward the newly enlarged shrine of James F. Drake on Fortieth Street. Here we encountered our friends the two Messrs. Drake, junior, and complimented them on their thews and sinews, these two gentlemen having recently, unaided, succeeded in moving a half-ton safe, filled with the treasures of Elizabethan literature, into the new sanctum. Here, where formerly sped the nimble fingers of M. Tappe's young ladies, busy with the compilation of engaging bonnets for the fair, now stand upon wine-dark shelves the rich gold and amber of fine bindings. We were moved by this sight. We said in our heart, we will erect a small madrigal upon this theme, entitled: "Song Upon Certain Songbirds of the Elizabethan Age Now Garnishing the Chamber Erstwhile Bright With the Stuffed Plumage of the Milliner." To the Messrs. Drake we mentioned the interesting letter of Mr. J. Acton Lomax in yesterday's *Tribune*, which called attention to the fact that the poem at the end of "Through the Looking Glass" is an acrostic giving the name of the original Alice—viz., Alice Pleasance Liddell. In return for which we were shown a copy of the first edition of "Alice in Wonderland." Here, too, we dallied for some time over a first edition of Dr. Johnson's Dictionary, and were pleased to learn that the great doctor was no more infallible in proofreading than the rest of us, one of our hosts pointing out to us a curious error by which some words beginning in COV had slipped in ahead of words beginning in COU.

*   *   *   *   *   *

Plum Pudding

AT NOON to-day we climbed on a Riverside Drive bus at Seventy-ninth Street and rode in the mellow gold of autumn up to Broadway and 168th. Serene, gilded weather; sunshine as soft and tawny as candlelight, genial at midday as the glow of an open fire in spite of the sharpness of the early morning. Battleships lay in the river with rippling flags. Men in flannels were playing tennis on the courts below Grant's Tomb; everywhere was a convincing appearance of comfort and prosperity. The beauty of the children, the good clothing of everybody, canes swinging on the pavements, cheerful faces untroubled by thought, the warm benevolence of sunlight, bronzing trees along Riverside Park, a man reading a book on the summit of that rounded knoll of rock near Eighty-fourth Street which children call "Mount Tom"—everything was so bright in life and vigour that the sentence seems to need no verb. Joan of Arc, poised on horseback against her screen of dark cedars, held her sword clearly against the pale sky. Amazingly sure and strong and established seem the rich façades of Riverside Drive apartment houses, and the landlords were rolling in limousines up to Claremont to have lunch. One small apartment house, near Eighty-third or thereabouts, has been renamed the Château-Thierry.

After crossing the long bridge above Claremont and the deep ravine where ships and ferryboats and coal stations abound, the bus crosses on 135th Street to Broadway. At 153d, the beautiful cemetery of Trinity Parish, leafy paths lying peaceful in the strong glow. At 166th Street is an open area now called Mitchel

Square, with an outcrop of rock polished by the rearward breeks of many sliding urchins. Some children
were playing on that small summit with a toy parachute
made of light paper and a pebble attached by threads.

On 168th Street alongside the big armoury of the
Twenty-second Engineers boys were playing base-
ball, with a rubber ball, pitching it so that the batter
received it on the bounce and struck it with his fist.
According to the score chalked on the pavement the
"Bronx Browns" and the "Haven Athletics" were
just finishing a rousing contest, in which the former
were victors, 1—0. Haven Avenue, near by, is a happy
little street perched high above the river. A small
terraced garden with fading flowers looks across the
Hudson to the woody Palisades. Modest apartment
houses are built high on enormous buttresses, over the
steep scarp of the hillside. Through cellar windows
coal was visible, piled high in the bins; children were
trooping home for dinner; a fine taint of frying onions
hung in the shining air. Everywhere in that open,
half-suburban, comfortable region was a feeling of sane,
established life. An old man with a white beard was
greeted by two urchins, who ran up and kissed him
heartily as he beamed upon them. Grandpa, one
supposes! Plenty of signs indicating small apartments
to rent, four and five rooms. And down that upper
slant of Broadway, as the bus bumbles past rows of
neat prosperous-seeming shops, one feels the great tug
and pulling current of life that flows down the channel,
the strange energy of the huge city lying below. The
tide was momentarily stilled, but soon to resume action.

Plum Pudding

There was a magic touch apparent, like the stillness of a palace in a fairy tale, bewitched into waiting silence.

*　　　　*　　　　*　　　　*　　　　*

SOMETIMES on our way to the office in the morning we stop in front of a jeweller's window near Maiden Lane and watch a neat little elderly gentleman daintily setting out his employer's gauds and trinkets for the day. We like to see him brood cheerfully over the disposition of his small amber-coloured velvet mats, and the arrangement of the rings, vanity cases, necklaces, and precious stones. They twinkle in the morning light, and he leans downward in the window, innocently displaying the widening parting on his pink scalp. He purses his lips in a silent whistle as he cons his shining trifles and varies his plan of display every day.

Now a modern realist (we have a painful suspicion) if he were describing this pleasant man would deal rather roughly with him. You know exactly how it would be done. He would be a weary, saddened, shabby figure: his conscientious attention to the jewels in his care would be construed as the painful and creaking routine of a victim of commercial greed; a bitter irony would be distilled from the contrast of his own modest station in life and the huge value of the lucid crystals and carbons under his hands. His hands—ah, the realist would angrily see some brutal pathos or unconscious naughtiness in the crook of the old mottled fingers. How that widening parting in the gray head would be gloated upon. It would be very easy to do, and it would be (if we are any judge) wholly false.

A City Note-book

For we have watched the little old gentleman many times, and we have quite an affection for him. We see him as one perfectly happy in the tidy and careful round of his tasks; and when his tenderly brushed gray poll leans above his treasures, and he gently devises new patterns by which the emeralds or the gold cigarette cases will catch the slant of 9 o'clock sunlight, we seem to see one who is enjoying his own placid conception of beauty, and who is not a figure of pity or reproach, but one of decent honour and excellent fidelity.

*　　　*　　　*　　　*　　　*

ONE of our colleagues, a lusty genial in respect of tobacco, has told us of a magnificent way to remove an evil and noisome taste from an old pipe that hath been smoked overlong. He says, clean the bowl carefully (not removing the cake) and wash tenderly in fair, warm water. Then, he says, take a teaspoonful of the finest vatted Scotch whiskey (or, if the pipe be of exceeding size, a tablespoonful of the same) and pour it delicately into the bowl. Apply a lighted match, and let the liquor burn itself out. It will do so, he avouches, with a gentle blue flame of great beauty and serenity. The action of this burning elixir, he maintains, operates to sizzle and purge away all impurity from the antique incrustation in the bowl. After letting the pipe cool, and then filling it with a favourite blend of mingled Virginia, Perique, and Latakia, our friend asserts that he is blessed with a cool, saporous, and enchanting fumigation which is so fragrant that even his wife has remarked upon it in terms compli-

[215]

mentary. Our friend says (but we fear he draws the longbow nigh unto fracture) that the success of this method may be tested so: if one lives, as he does, in the upward stories of a tall apartment house, one should take the pipe so cleansed to the window-sill, and, smoking it heartily, lean outward over the sill. On a clear, still, blue evening, the air being not too gusty, the vapours will disperse and eddy over the street; and he maintains with great zeal that passersby ten tiers below will very soon look upward from the pavement, sniffingly, to discern the source of such admirable fumes. He has even known them, he announces, to hail him from the street, in tones of eager inquiry, to learn what kind of tobacco he is smoking.

All this we have duly meditated and find ourselves considerably stirred. Now there is only one thing that stands between ourself and such an experiment.

*　　　*　　　*　　　*　　　*

THERE are some who hold by the theory that on visiting a restaurant it is well to pick out a table that is already cleared rather than one still bearing the débris of a previous patron's meal. We offer convincing proof to the contrary.

Rambling, vacant of mind and guileless of intent, in a certain quiet portion of the city—and it is no use for you, O client, to ask where, for our secrecy is firm as granite—we came upon an eating house and turned inward. There were tables spread with snowy cloths, immaculate; there were also tables littered with dishes. We chose one of the latter, for a waiter was removing

the plates, and we thought that by sitting there we
would get prompter service. We sat down and our
eye fell upon a large china cup that had been used by
the preceding luncher. In the bottom of that cup was
a little pool of dark dregs, a rich purple colour, most
agreeable to gaze upon. Happy possibilities were
opened to our mind. Like the fabled Captain X, we
had a Big Idea. We made no outcry, nor did we show
our emotion, but when the waiter asked for our order
we said, calmly: "Sausages and some of the red wine."
He was equally calm and uttered no comment.

Soon he came back (having conferred, as we could
see out of the wing of our eye) with his boss. "What
was it you ordered?" he said.

"Sausages," we replied, urbanely, "and some of the
red wine."

"I don't remember having served you before," he
said. "I can't give you anything like that."

We saw that we must win his confidence and we
thought rapidly. "It's perfectly all right," we said.
"Mr. Bennett" (we said, seizing the first name that
came into our head), "who comes here every day, told
me about it. You know Mr. Bennett; he works over
on Forty-second Street and comes here right along."

Again he departed, but returned anon with smiling
visage. "If you're a friend of Mr. Bennett's," he said,
"it's all right. You know, we have to be careful."

"Quite right," we said; "be wary." And we laid
hand firmly on the fine hemorrhage of the grape.

A little later in the adventure, when we were asked
what dessert we would have, we found stewed rhubarb

on the menu, and very fine stewed rhubarb it was;
wherefore we say that our time was not ill-spent and we
shall keep the secret to ourself.

But we can't help feeling grateful to Mr. Bennett,
whoever he is.

*　　　*　　　*　　　*　　　*

OCCASIONALLY (but not often) in the exciting plexus
of our affairs (conducted, as we try to persuade ourself, with so judicious a jointure of caution and hilarity) we find it necessary to remain in town for dinner.
Then, and particularly in spring evenings, we are moved
and exhilarated by that spectacle that never loses its enchantment, the golden beauty and glamour of downtown New York after the homeward ebb has left the
streets quiet and lonely. By six o'clock in a May
sunset the office is a cloister of delicious peace and solitude. Let us suppose (oh, a case merely hypothetic)
that you have got to attend a dinner somewhere in the
Forties, say at half-past seven; and it is requisite that
evening clothes should be worn. You have brought
them to the office, modestly hidden, in a bag; and in
that almost unbelievable privacy, toward half-past
six, you have an enjoyable half hour of luxurious amusement and contemplation. The office, one repeats, is
completely stripped of tenants—save perhaps an occasional grumbling sortie by the veteran janitor. So
all its resources are open for you to use as boudoir.
Now, in an office situated like this there is, at sunset
time, a variety of scenic richness to be contemplated.
From the President's office (putting on one's hard-

A City Note-book

boiled shirt) one can look down upon St. Paul's church-yard, lying a pool of pale blue shadow in the rising dusk. From the City Room (inserting studs) one sees the river sheeted with light. From the office of the Literary Editor (lacing up one's shoes) one may study the wild pinnacle of Woolworth, faintly superfused with a brightness of gold and pink. From the office of one of our dramatic critics the view is negligible (being but a hardy brick wall), but the critic, debonair creature, has a small mirror of his own, so there one manages the ticklish business of the cravat. And from our own kennel, where are transacted the last touches (transfer of pipe, tobacco, matches, Long Island railroad timetable, commutation ticket, etc., to the other pockets) there is a heavenly purview of those tall cliffs of lower Broadway, nobly terraced into the soft, translucent sky. In that exquisite clarity and sharpness of New York's evening light are a loveliness and a gallantry hardly to be endured. At seven o'clock of a May evening it is poetry unspeakable. O magnificent city (one says), there will come a day when others will worship and celebrate your mystery; and when not one of them will know or care how much I loved you. But these words, obscure and perishable, I leave you as a testimony that I also understood.

She cannot be merely the cruel Babel they like to describe her: the sunset light would not gild her so tenderly.

*　　　*　　　*　　　*　　　*

It was a great relief to us yesterday evening to see a man reading a book in the subway. We have undergone so many embarrassments trying to make out the titles of the books the ladies read, without running afoul of the Traveller's Aid Society, that we heaved a sigh of relief and proceeded to stalk our quarry with a light heart. Let us explain that on a crowded train it is not such an easy task. You see your victim at the other end of the car. First you have to buffet your way until you get next to him. Then, just as you think you are in a position to do a little careful snooping, he innocently shifts the book to the other hand. This means you have got to navigate, somehow, toward the hang-handle on the other side of him. Very well. By the time the train gets to Bowling Green we have seen that it is a fattish book, bound in green cloth, and the author's name begins with FRAN. That doesn't help much. As the train roars under the river you manage, by leanings and twistings, to see the publisher's name—in this case, Longmans. At Borough Hall a number of passengers get out, and the hunted reader sits down. Ten to one he will hold the book in such a way that you cannot see the title. At Nevins Street you get a seat beside him. At Atlantic Avenue, as he is getting off, you propose your head over his shoulder in the jam on the stairs and see what you are after. "Lychgate Hall," by M. E. Francis. And in this case, success left us none the wiser.

Atlantic Avenue, by the way, always seems to us an ideal place for the beginning of a detective story. (Speaking of that, a very jolly article in this month's *Bookman*, called "How Old Is Sherlock Holmes?" has revived our old ambition to own a complete set of

A City Note-book

all the Sherlock Holmes tales, and we are going to set about scouring the town for them). Every time we pass through the Atlantic Avenue maelstrom, which is twelve times a week, we see, as plain as print, the beginning of two magazine tales.

One begins as the passengers are streaming through the gate toward the 5:27 train. There is a very beautiful damsel who always sits on the left-hand side of the next to last car, by an open window. On her plump and comely white hand, which holds the latest issue of a motion picture magazine, is a sparkling diamond ring. Suddenly all the lights in the train go out. Through the open window comes a brutal grasp which wrenches the bauble from her finger. There are screams, etc., etc. When the lights go on again, of course there is no sign of the criminal. Five minutes later, Mr. Geoffrey Dartmouth, enjoying a chocolate ice cream soda in the little soft-drink alcove at the corner of the station, is astonished to find a gold ring, the stone missing, at the bottom of his paper soda container.

The second story begins on the Atlantic Avenue platform of the Lexington Avenue subway. It is 9 A. M., and a crowded train is pulling out. Just before the train leaves a young man steps off one of the cars, leaving behind him (though not at once noticed) a rattan suitcase. This young man disappears in the usual fashion, viz., by mingling with the crowd. When the train gets to the end of the run the unclaimed suitcase is opened, and found to contain—*continued on page* 186.

continued on page 186.

*   *   *   *   *

Plum Pudding

EVERY now and then we take a stroll up Irving Place. It is changing slowly, but it still has much of the flavour that Arthur Maurice had in mind when he christened it "the heart of O. Henry land." Number 55, the solid, bleached brownstone house where O. Henry once lived, is still there: it seems to be some sort of ecclesiastical rendezvous, if one may judge by the letters C. H. A. on the screen and the pointed carving of the doorway. Number 53, next door, always interests us greatly: the windows give a glimpse of the most extraordinary number of cages of canaries.

The old German theatre seems to have changed its language: the boards speak now in Yiddish. The chiropractor and psycho-analyst has invaded the Place, as may be seen by a sign on the eastern side. O. Henry would surely have told a yarn about him if he had been there fifteen years ago. There are still quite a number of the old brown houses, with their iron railings and little patches of grass. The chocolate factory still diffuses its pleasant candied whiff. At noontime the street is full of the high-spirited pupils of the Washington Irving High School. As for the Irving house itself, it is getting a new coat of paint. The big corset works, we dare say, has come since O. Henry's time. We had quite an adventure there once. We can't remember how it came about, but for some reason or other we went to that building to see the chief engineer. All we can remember about it was that he had been at sea at one time, and we went to see him on some maritime errand. We found that he and his family lived in a comfortable apartment on the roof of the factory, and we remember making our way, with a good many blushes, through several hundred or thousand young ladies who were industriously working away at their employer's business and who seemed to us to be giggling more than necessary. After a good deal of hunting we found our way to a secret stair and reached our seafaring engineer of the corset factory in his eyrie, where (we remember) there were oil paintings of ships on the walls and his children played about on the roof as though on the deck of a vessel.

Irving Place is also very rich in interesting little shops—laundries, tailors, carpenters, stationers, and a pleasant bookshop. It is a haunt of hand-organ men. The cool tavern at the corner of Eighteenth, where Con Delaney tended the bar in the days when O. Henry visited it, is there still. All along the little byway is a calm, genteel, domestic mood, in spite of the encroachments of factories and apartment houses. There are window boxes with flowers, and a sort of dim suffusion of conscious literary feeling. One has a suspicion that in all those upper rooms are people writing short stories. "Want to see a freak?" asks the young man in the bookshop as we are looking over his counters. We do, of course, and follow his animated gesture. Across the street comes a plump young woman, in a very short skirt of a violent blue, with a thick mane of bobbed hair, carrying her hat in her hand. She looks rather comfortable and seemly to us, but something about her infuriates the bookseller. He is quite Freudian in his indignation that any young woman should habit herself so. We wonder what the psycho-analyst a few blocks below would say about it. And walking a few paces further, one comes upon the green twitter, the tended walks and pink geranium beds of Gramercy Park.

* * * * *

THERE is no time when we need spiritual support so much as when we are having our hair cut, for indeed it is the only time when we are ever thoroughly and entirely Bored. But having found a good-natured barber who said he would not mind our reading a book while he was shearing, we went through with it. The ideal book to read at such a time (we offer you this advice, brave friends) is the "Tao" of Lao-Tse, that ancient and admirable Chinese sage. (Dwight Goddard's translation is very agreeable.) "The Tao," as of course you know, is generally translated The Way, i. e., the Way of Life of the Reasonable Man.

Lao-Tse, we assert, is the ideal author to read while the barber is at his business. He answers every inquiry that will be made, and all you have to do is hold the book up and point to your favourite marked passages.

When the barber says, genially, "Well, have you done your Christmas shopping yet?" we raise the book and point to this maxim:

> *Taciturnity is natural to man.*

When he says, "How about a nice little shampoo this morning?" we are prompt to indicate:

> *The wise man attends to the inner significance of things and does not concern himself with outward appearances.*

A City Note-book

When, as we sit in the chair, we see (in the mirror before us) the lovely reflection of the beautiful manicure lady, and she arches her eyebrows at us to convey the intimation that we ought to have our hands attended to, old Lao-Tse is ready with the answer. We reassure ourself with his remark:

Though he be surrounded with sights that are magnificent, the wise man will remain calm and unconcerned.

When the shine boy offers to burnish our shoes, we call his attention to:

He who closes his mouth and shuts his sense gates will be free from trouble to the end of life.

When the barber suggests that if we were now to have a liberal douche of bay rum sprayed over our poll it would be a glittering consummation of his task, we show him the words:

If one tries to improve a thing, he mars it.

And when (finally) the irritated tonsor suggests that if we don't wait so long next time before getting our hair cut we will not be humiliated by our condition, we exhibit Lao-Tse's aphorism:

The wise man is inaccessible to favour or hate; he cannot be reached by profit or injury; he cannot be honoured or humiliated.

"It's very easy," says the barber as we pay our check; "just drop in here once a month and we'll fix you up." And we point to:

Plum Pudding

The wise man lives in the world, but he lives cautiously, dealing with the world cautiously. Many things that appear easy are full of difficulties.

*　　　*　　　*　　　*　　　*

To a lot of people who are in a mortal scurry and excitement what is so maddening as the calm and unruffled serenity of a dignified philosopher who gazes unperturbed upon their pangs? So did we meditate when facing the deliberate and mild tranquillity of the priestly person presiding over the bulletin board announcing the arrival of trains at the Pennsylvania Station. It was in that desperate and curious limbo known as the "exit concourse," where baffled creatures wait to meet others arriving on trains and maledict the architect who so planned matters that the passengers arrive on two sides at once, so that one stands grievously in the middle slewing his eyes to one side and another in a kind of vertigo, attempting to con both exits. We cannot go into this matter in full (when, indeed, will we find enough white paper and enough energy to discuss *anything* in full, in the way, perhaps, Henry James would have blanketed it?), but we will explain that we were waiting to meet someone, someone we had never seen, someone of the opposite sex and colour, in short, that rare and desirable creature a cook, imported from another city, and she had missed her train, and all we knew was her first name and that she would wear a "brown turban." After prowling distraitly round the station (and a large station it is) and asking every likely person if her name was Amanda, and being frowned upon and suspected as a black slaver, and thinking we felt on our neck the heated breath and handcuffs of the Travellers' Aid Society, we decided that Amanda must have missed her train and concluded to wait for the next. Then it was, to return to our thesis, that we had occasion to observe and feel in our own person the wretched pangs of one in despair facing the gentle—shall we say hesychastic?—peace and benevolent quietness of the man at the bulletin board. Bombarded with questions by the impatient and anxious crowd, with what pacific good nature he answered our doubts and querulities. And yet how irritating was his calmness, his deliberation, the very placidity of his mien as he surveyed his clacking telautograph and leisurely took out his schoolroom eraser, rubbed off an inscription, then polished the board with a cloth, then looked for a piece of chalk and wrote in a fine curly hand some notation about a train from Cincinnati in which we were not at all interested. Ah, here we are at last! Train from Philadelphia! Arriving on track Number—; no, wrong again! He only changes 5 *minutes late* to 10 *minutes late*. The crowd mutters and fumes. The telautograph begins to stutter and we gaze at it feverishly. It stops again and our dominie looks at it calmly. He taps it gently with his finger. We wonder, is it out of order? Perhaps that train is already coming in and he doesn't know it, and Amanda may be wandering lost somewhere in the vast vistas of the station looking for us. Shall we dash up to the waiting room and have another look? But Amanda does not know the station, and there are so many places where benches are put, and she might think one of those was the waiting room that had been mentioned. And then there is this Daylight Saving time mix-up. In a sudden panic we cannot figure out whether Philadelphia time is an hour ahead of New York time or an hour behind. We told Amanda to take the one o'clock from Philadelphia. Well, should she arrive here at two o'clock or at four? It being now 5:10 by our time, what are we to do? The telautograph clicks. The priestly person slowly and gravely writes down that the Philadelphia train is arriving on Track 6. There is a mad rush: everyone dashes to the gate. And here, coming up the stairs, is a coloured lady whose anxiously speculating eye must be the one we seek. In the mutuality of our worry we recognize each other at once. We seize her in triumph; in fact, we could have embraced her. All our anguish is past. Amanda is ours!

THOUGHTS IN THE SUBWAY

I

WE HEAR people complain about the subway: its brutal competitive struggle, its roaring fury and madness. We think they have not sufficiently considered it.

Any experience shared daily and for a long time by a great many people comes to have a communal and social importance; it is desirable to fill it with meaning and see whether there may not be some beauty in it. The task of civilization is not to be always looking wistfully back at a Good Time long ago, or always panting for a doubtful millennium to come; but to see the significance and secret of that which is around us. And so we say, in full seriousness, that for one observer at any rate the subway is a great school of human study. We will not say that it is an easy school: it is no kindergarten; the curriculum is strenuous and wearying, and not always conducive to blithe cheer.

But what a tide of humanity, poured to and fro in great tides over which the units have little control. What a sharp and troubled awareness of our fellow-beings, drawn from study of those thousands of faces—the fresh living beauty of the girls, the faces of men empty of all but suffering and disillusion, a shabby errand boy asleep, goggling with weariness and adenoids —so they go crashing through the dark in a patient fellowship of hope and mysterious endurance. How can one pass through this quotidian immersion in humanity without being, in some small degree, enriched by that admiring pity which is the only emotion that can permanently endure under the eye of a questioning star?

Why, one wonders, should we cry out at the pangs and scuffles of the subway? Do we expect great things to come to pass without corresponding suffering? Some day a great poet will be born in the subway—spiritually speaking; one great enough to show us the terrific and savage beauty of this multitudinous miracle. As one watches each of those passengers, riding with some inscrutable purpose of his own (or an even more inscrutable lack of purpose) toward duty or liberation, he may be touched with anger and contempt toward individuals; but he must admit the majesty of the spectacle in the mass. One who loves his country for a certain candour and quick vigour of spirit will view the scene again and again in the hope of spying out some secrets of the national mind and destiny. Daily he bathes in America. He has that curious sense of mystical meaning in common things that a traveller feels coming home from abroad, when he finds even the most casual glimpses strangely pregnant with national identity. In the advertisements, despite all their absurdities; in voices humorous or sullen; even in the books that the girls are reading (for most girls read books in the subway) he will try to divine some authentic law of life.

He is but a poor and mean-spirited lover—whether of his city, his country, or anything else—who loves her only because he has known no other. We are shy of vociferating patriotism because it is callow and empty, sprung generally from mere ignorance. The true enthusiast, we would like to think, is he who can travel daily some dozen or score of miles in the subway, plunged in the warm wedlock of the rush hours; and can still gather some queer loyalty to that rough, drastic experience. Other than a sense of pity and affection toward those strangely sculptured faces, all busy upon the fatal tasks of men, it is hard to be precise as to just what he has learned. But as the crowd pours from the cars, and shrugs off the burden of the journey, you may see them looking upward to console themselves with perpendicular loveliness leaping into the clear sky. Ah, they are well trained. All are oppressed and shackled by things greater than themselves; yet within their own orbits of free movement they are masters of the event. They are patient and friendly, and endlessly brave.

II

The train roared through the subway, that warm typhoon whipping light summer dresses in a multitudinous flutter. All down the bright crowded aisle of patient humanity I could see their blowing colours.

My eyes were touched with Truth: I saw them as they are, beautiful and brave.

Is Time never sated with loveliness? How many million such he has devoured, and must he take these, too? They are so young, so slender, so untutored, such unconscious vessels of amazing life; so courageous in their simple finery, so unaware of the Enemy that waits for us all. With what strange cruelties will he trouble them, their very gayety a temptation to his hand? See them on Broadway at the lunch hour, pouring in their vivacious thousands onto the pavement. Is there no one who wonders about these merry little hostages? Can you look on them without marvelling at their gallant mien?

They are aware of their charms, but unconscious of their loveliness. Surely they are a new generation of their sex, cool, assured, even capable. They are happy, because they do not think too much; they are lovely, because they are so perishable, because (despite their naïve assumption of certainty) one knows them so delightfully only an innocent ornament of this business world of which they are so ignorant. They are the cheerful children of Down Town, and Down Town looks upon them with the affectionate compassion children merit. Their joys, their tragedies, are the emotions of children—all the more terrible for that reason.

And so you see them, day after day, blithely and gallantly faring onward in this Children's Crusade. Can you see that caravan of life without a pang? For many

Thoughts in the Subway

it is tragic to be young and beautiful and a woman.
Luckily, they do not know it, and they never will. But
in courage, and curiosity, and loveliness, how they put
us all to shame. I see them, flashing by in a subway
train, golden sphinxes, whose riddles (as Mr. Cabell said
of Woman) are not worth solving. Yet they are all the
more appealing for that fact. For surely to be a
riddle which is not worth solving, and still is cherished
as a riddle, is the greatest mystery of all. What
strange journeys lie before them, and how triumphantly
they walk the precipices as though they were mere
meadow paths.

My eyes were touched with Truth, and I saw them as
they are, beautiful and brave. And sometimes I think
that even Time must be sated with loveliness; that he
will not crumble them or mar their gallant childishness;
that he will leave them, their bright dresses fluttering, as
I have seem them in the subway many a summer day.

DEMPSEY vs. CARPENTIER

THE race is not to the swift, nor the battle to the strong; but as Frank Adams once remarked, the betting is best that way. The event at Boyle's Thirty Acres in Jersey City was the conclusive triumph of Reality over Romance, of Prose over Poetry. To almost all the newspaper-reading world—except the canny fellows who study these matters with care and knowledge—Carpentier had taken on something of the lustre and divinity of myth. He was the white Greek god, he was Mercury and Apollo. The dope was against him; but there were many who felt, obscurely, that in some pregnant way a miracle would happen. His limbs were ivory, his eyes were fire; surely the gods would intervene! Perhaps they would have but for the defi-

[234]

nite pronouncement of the mystagogue G. B. Shaw.
Even the gods could not resist the chance of catching
Shaw off his base.

We are not a turncoat; we had hoped that Carpentier would win. It would have been pleasant if
he had, quite like a fairy tale. But we must tell
things as we see them. Dempsey, in a very difficult
situation, bore himself as a champion, and (more than
that) as a man of spirit puzzled and angered by the
feeling that has been rumoured against him. Carpentier entered the ring smiling, perfectly at ease; but there
was that same sunken, wistful, faintly weary look
about his eyes that struck us when we first saw him,
at Manhasset, three weeks ago. It was the look of a
man who has had more put upon him than he can
rightly bear. But with what a grace and aplomb he
stood upon that scaffold! Dempsey, on the other hand,
was sullen and sombre; when they spoke together he
seemed embarrassed and kept his face averted. As the
hands were bandaged and gloves put on, he sat with
lowered head, his dark poll brooding over his fists,
not unlike Rodin's Thinker. Carpentier, at the opposite corner, was apparently at ease; sat smilingly in his
gray and black gown, watching the airplanes.

You have read the accounts of the fight to small
purpose if you do not realize that Carpentier was utterly outclassed—not in skill or cunning, but in those
qualities where the will has no part, in power and reach.
From the first clinch, when Dempsey began that series
of terrible body jabs that broke down the Frenchman's
energy and speed, the goose was cooked. There was

nothing poetic or glamorous about those jabs; they were not spectacular, not particularly swift; but they were terribly definite. Half a dozen of them altered the scene strangely. The smiling face became haggard and troubled.

Carpentier, too, must have been leaving something to the gods, for his tactics were wildly reckless. He was the aggressor at the start, leading fiercely for Dempsey's jaw, and landing, too, but not heavily enough to do damage. Again and again in that first round he fell into the fatal embrace in which Dempsey punished him busily, with those straight body strokes that slid in methodically, like pistons. Georges seemed to have no defence that could slacken those blows. After every clinch his strength plainly ebbed and withered. Away, he dodged nimbly, airily, easily more dramatic in arts of manœuvre. But Dempsey, tall, sullen, composed, followed him steadily. He seemed slow beside that flying white figure, but that wheeling amble was deadly sure. He was always on the inner arc, Carpentier on the outer; the long, swarthy arms were impenetrable in front of his vitals; again and again he followed up, seeking to corner his man; Carpentier would fling a shining arm at the dark jaw; a clinch would follow in which the two leaned together in that curious posture of apparent affection; and they hung upon each other's necks—Carpentier, from a distance, looking almost like a white girl languishing in the arms of some dark, solicitous lover. But Mr. Dempsey was the Fatal Bridegroom, for at each union he would rivet in several more of those steam punches.

Dempsey *vs.* Carpentier

There was something almost incredible in the scene—
so we had been drilled in that Million-Dollar Myth, the
unscathability of Carpentier. Was this Gorgeous
Georges, this blood-smeared, wilting, hunted figure,
flitting desperately from the grim, dark-jowled avenger?
And then, in the latter part of the second round,
Georges showed one flash of his true genius. Suddenly
he sprang, leaping (so it seemed) clear from the canvas,
and landed solidly (though not killingly) on Dempsey's
jaw. There was a flicker of lightning blows, and for
an instant Dempsey was retreating, defensive, even a
little jarred. That was the high moment of the fight,
and the crowd then showed its heart. Ninety thousand
people had come there to see bloodshed; through several
humid hours they had sat in a rising temperature, both
inward and outward, with cumulating intensity like that
of a kettle approaching the boil. Dempsey had had a
bigger hand on entering the ring; but so far it had
been too one-sided for much roaring. But now, for an
instant, there was actual fighting. There were some
who thought that if Georges could have followed up this
advantage he still had a chance. We do not think so.
Dempsey was not greatly shaken. He was too powerful and too hard to reach. They clinched and stalled
for a moment, and the gong came shortly. But Carpentier had shown his tiger streak. Scotty Monteith,
manager (so we were told) of Johnny Dundee, sat just
in front of us in a pink skirt, and had been gathering up
substantial wagers from the ill-starred French journalists near by. Scotty was not in any doubt as to the out-
come, but even he was moved by Carpentier's gallant

sally. "No one knew he was a fighter like that," he said.

The rest is but a few words. Carpentier's face had a wild, driven look. His hits seemed mere taps beside Dempsey's. In the fourth round he went down once, for eight or nine counts, and climbed up painfully. The second time he sprawled flat; Dempsey, still with that pensive lowered head, walked grimly in a semi-circle, waiting to see if that was the end. It was. Greek gods are no match for Tarzans in this game.

It was all over in a breathless flash. It was not one lucky blow that did it, but a sequence of business-like crushing strokes. We shall not soon forget that picture before the gong rang: Carpentier, still the White Knight of legend and glory, with his charming upward smile and easy unconcern; and Dempsey's dark cropped head, bent and glowering over his chest. There was in Dempsey's inscrutable, darkling mien a cold, simmering anger, as of a man unfairly hounded, he hardly knew why. And probably, we think, un-justly. You will say that we import a symbolism into a field where it scarcely thrives. But Carpentier's en-gaging merriment in the eye of oncoming downfall seemed to us almost a parable of those who have smiled too confidingly upon the dark faces of the gods.

A LETTER TO A SEA CAPTAIN

(To D.W.B.)

DEAR CAPTAIN:

You are the most modest of men, but even at the
risk of arousing your displeasure we have it on our
mind to say something about you. We shall try not to
be offensively personal, for indeed we are thinking not
merely of yourself but also of the many others of your
seafaring art who have always been such steadfast ser-
vants of the public, the greatness of whose service has
not always been well enough understood. But perhaps
it is only fair that the sea captain, so unquestionable
an autocrat in his own world, should be called upon to
submit to that purging and erratic discipline which is
so notable a feature of our American life—publicity!

Plum Pudding

It is not enough understood, we repeat, how valuable and charming the sea captain is as an agent and private ambassador of international friendship. Perhaps we do not know you until we have seen you at sea (may the opportunity serve anon!). We have only known you with your majesty laid aside, your severity relaxed. But who else so completely and humorously understands both sides of the water, and in his regular movements from side to side acts so shrewd a commentator on Anglo-American affairs? Who takes more keen delight in our American ways, in the beauty of this New York of which we are so proud, who has done so much to endear each nation to the other? Yours, true to your blood (for you are *Scot Scotorum*), is the humorist's way: how many passengers you have warmed and tickled with your genial chaff, hiding constant kindness under a jocose word, perhaps teasing us Americans on our curious conduct of knives and forks, or (for a change) taking the cisatlantic side of the jape, esteeming no less highly a sound poke at British foibles.

All this is your personal gift: it is no necessary part of the master's equipment to be so gracefully conversable. Of the graver side of the sea captain's life, though you say little, we see it unconsciously written in your bearing. Some of us, who know just a little about it, can guess something of its burdens, its vigils, and its courages. There is something significant in the obscure instinct that some of your friends have to seize what opportunity they can of seeing you in your own quarters when you are in port. For though a ship in dock is a ship fettered and broken of much of her life

A Letter to a Sea Captain

and meaning, yet in the captain's cabin the landsman feels something of that fine, faithful, and rigorous way of life. It is a hard life, he knows; a life of stringent seriousness, of heavy responsibilities: and yet it is a life for which we are fool enough to speak the fool's word of envy. It is a life spared the million frittering interruptions and cheerful distractions that devil the journalist; it is a life cut down to the essentials of discipline, simplicity, and service; a life where you must, at necessity, be not merely navigator but magistrate, employer, and priest. Birth, death, and all the troubles that lie between, fall under your sway, and must find you unperturbed. But, when you go out of that snug cabin for your turn of duty, at any rate you have the dark happiness of knowing that you go to a struggle worthy your powers, the struggle with that old, immortal, unconquerable, and yet daily conquered enemy, the Sea.

And so you go and come, you go and come, and we learn to count on your regular appearance every four weeks as we would on any stated gesture of the zodiac. You come eager to pick up the threads of what has been happening in this our town, what books people are talking about, what is the latest jape, and what (your tastes being so catholic!) "Percy and Ferdie" are up to. And you, in turn, bring news of what they are saying in Sauchiehall Street or Fleet Street, and what books are making a stir on the other side. You take copies of American books that catch your fancy and pass them on to British reviewers, always at your quixotic task of trying to make each side appreciate the other's humours. For, though we promised not to give you away too personally, you are not only the sea captain but the man of letters, too, eminent in that field in your own right.

There must be some valid reason why so many good writers, and several who have some claim on the word "great," have been bred of the sea. Great writing comes from great stress of mind—which even a journalist may suffer—but it also requires strictness of seclusion and isolation. Surely, on the small and decently regimented island of a ship a man's mind must turn inward. Surrounded by all that barren beauty of sky and sea, so lovely, and yet so meaningless to the mind, the doomed business of humanity must seem all the more precious and deserving of tenderness. Perhaps that is what old George Herbert meant when he said, *He that will learn to pray, let him go to sea.*

THE END

A modern humorist with the tang of an Elizabethan

CHRISTOPHER MORLEY

ONCE upon a time Christopher Morley was coerced, against the objections of a well-nigh blushing modesty, to dictate some notes which we may go so far as to call autobiographical. In part they were:

"Born at Haverford, Pa., in 1890; father, professor of mathematics and a poet; mother a musician, poet, and fine cook. I was handicapped by intellectual society and good nourishment. I am and always have been too well fed. Great literature proceeds from an empty stomach. My proudest achievement is having been asked by a college president to give a course of lectures on Chaucer.

"When I was graduated from Haverford in 1910, a benevolent posse of college presidents in Maryland sent me to New College, Oxford, as a Rhodes scholar. At Oxford I learned to drink shandygaff. When I came home from England in 1913 I started to work for Doubleday, Page & Company at Garden City. I learned to read Conrad, and started my favorite hobby, which is getting letters from William McFee. By the way, my favorite amusement is hanging around Leary's second-hand book store in Philadelphia. My dearest dream is to own some kind of a boat, write one good novel and about thirty plays which would each run a year on Broadway. I have written book reviews, editorials, dramatic notices, worked as a reporter, a librarian, in a bookstore, and have given lectures." Mr. Morley should have added that he is now conductor of "The Bowling Green" on the editorial page of the New York *Evening Post.*

PLUM PUDDING

By CHRISTOPHER MORLEY

"And merrily embellished by Walter Jack Duncan"

THUS Mr. Morley entitles his new volume, in which he has occupied himself with books in particular, but also with divers other ingredients such as city and suburban incidents, women, dogs, children, tadpoles, and so on.

Plum Pudding, $1.75

THE HAUNTED BOOKSHOP

WE HAVE just found an advertisement for "The Haunted Bookshop" which was never released, though it was written before the book was published. Can you guess the writer of it? We're not at liberty to tell, for he would never forgive our mentioning his name.

"THIS SHOP IS HAUNTED!"

Such was the sign that met the eyes of those who entered *Parnassus at Home*, a very unusual bookshop on Gissing Street, Brooklyn. Roger Mifflin, the eccentric booklover who owned the shop, only meant that his shop was haunted by the great spirits of literature, but there were more substantial ghosts about, as the story tells. Read the curious adventures that befell after Titania Chapman came to learn the book business in the mellow atmosphere of the second-hand bookshop of this novel. There was mystery connected with the elusive copy of Carlyle's *Oliver Cromwell*, which kept on disappearing from Roger's shelves. Some readers may remember that Roger Mifflin was the hero of Mr. Morley's first novel, *Parnassus on Wheels*, though this is in no sense a sequel, but an independent story.

The Haunted Bookshop, $1.75

SHANDYGAFF

This is the book at the beginning of which its author has placed this bit of explanation:

> *SHANDYGAFF*: a very refreshing drink, being a mixture of bitter ale or beer and ginger-beer, commonly drunk by the lower classes of England, and by strolling tinkers, low church parsons, newspaper men, journalists, and prizefighters. . . .
>
> JOHN MISTLETOE:
> *Dictionary of Deplorable Facts*

Published in the war period, "Shandygaff" brought this humorous letter from J. Edgar Park, of Massachusetts, Presbyterian pastor and author of "The Disadvantages of Being Good":

"This book of Morley's is absolutely useless—mere rot. It has already cost me not only its price but also two candles for an all-night séance and an entire degeneration of my most sad and sober resolutions. Money I needed for shoes, solemnity I needed for my reputation—all have gone to the winds in this nightmare of love, laughter, boyishness, and tobacco-smoke!"   *Shandygaff, $1.75*

PIPEFULS

"These sketches gave me pain to write; they will give the judicious patron pain to read; therefore we are quits. I think, as I look over their slattern paragraphs, of that most tragic hour—it falls about 4 P. M. in the office of an evening newspaper—when the unhappy compiler tries to round up the broodings of the day and still get home in time for supper."

The Author

"Envelops in clouds of fragrant English many quaint ideas about life, living, and literature . . . A belated Elizabethan who has strayed into the twentieth century! These piping little essays are mellow and leisurely!"—*The Sun*, New York   *Pipefuls, $1.75*

KATHLEEN—*a story*

"Kathleen" is about an Oxford undergraduate prank. Members of a literary club, *The Scorpions*, agree to write a serial story on shares. They invent a tale around certain names in an accidentally found letter signed "Kathleen." Their romantic fervor soon takes them off together in search of the real author of the letter. One suspects that Mr. Morley, as a Rhodes scholar at Oxford, might have been up to just such pranks. Anyway, consider this dedication: "TO THE REAL KATHLEEN—*With Apologies.*" His comedy is as interesting as his essays, its humor pointed by the rapid flow of action.

Kathleen, $1.25

TALES FROM A ROLLTOP DESK

The lucky eleven stories in this volume are introduced by a long letter of dedication which starts off:

DEAR EFFENDI:

I take the liberty of dedicating these little stories to you, with affection and respect. They have all grown, in one mood or another, out of the various life of Grub Street, suggested by adventures with publishers, booksellers, magazine editors, newspaper men, theatrical producers, commuters, and poets major and minor. If they have any appeal at all it must be as an honest (though perhaps too jocular) picture of the excitements that gratify the career of young men who embark upon the ocean of ink, and (let us not forget) those much-enduring Titanias who consent to share their vicissitudes. . . .

You must be sure to read the rest of this delightful letter before you start the first story in the book.

Tales From a Rolltop Desk, $1.75

PARNASSUS ON WHEELS

Was this book one of the innumerable manuscripts Morley nurtured in his personal plans for publishing, when he visited his first employer asking for a job? This incident is described reminiscently by that employer as follows (excerpt): "Morley immediately dove into a deep pocket and produced a large number of papers on which were worked out books and plans for series of books in vast array. To gain time, I suggested that to work out these schemes would almost break the Chemical Bank. But I failed to interest him. He had it in his mind that he had come to a publisher to talk books—not finance—a subject which, so far as I have been able to see, Morley found rather boresome then and since!"

After "Parnassus on Wheels" appeared, Edwin F. Edgett (Boston *Evening Transcript*) wrote: "To read 'Parnassus on Wheels' is to be glad there are books in the world. It gives us hope for the younger generation of writers!"

Parnassus on Wheels, $1.50

Morley's popularity explains our addition of three more titles to the limp leather edition of his works. Now available in pocket size, red leather binding: The Haunted Bookshop, Parnassus on Wheels, Shandygaff, Pipefuls, Plum Pudding, $2.50 each; the set, $12.50.

The Publishers